More Than Graphs

Mathematical Explorations for
TI-73, TI-82, TI-83, and TI-83 Plus Graphing Calculators

Revised and Updated

Jim Specht

KEY CURRICULUM PRESS
Innovators in Mathematics Education

ocm 45200415

Project Editor: Crystal Mills
Project Administrators: Jeff Gammon and Laurie Medeiros
Editorial Consultant: Pamela Harris
Production Editor: Deborah Cogan
Copy Editor: Margaret Moore
Production Coordinator: Alan Watt
Production and Manufacturing Manager: Diana Jean Parks
Text Designer, Compositor, and Illustrator: Joe Spooner
Cover Designer: Rick Helf

Executive Editor: Casey FitzSimons
Publisher: Steven Rasmussen

Special thanks to: Dr. Bernard Grofman (*Modeling Jury Verdicts*), Tom Stone (*Decaying M&Ms®*), Dr. Chuck VonderEmbse (*Circle Graphs*), Rick Jennings (*Shape Shifter*), and Mike Contino (*Circle Graphs, The Chaos Game,* and *Polygon π*)

Key Curriculum Press
1150 65th Street
Emeryville, CA 94608
510-595-7000
editorial@keypress.com
http://www.keypress.com

Printed in the United States of America
10 9 8 7 6 5 4   11 10 09
ISBN 978-1-55953-400-0

CONTENTS

About the author

Jim Specht has more than 25 years of experience as a teacher at both high schools and middle schools. He is a past president of the Oregon Council of Teachers of Mathematics and presents professional development activities to support other teachers currently in the classroom. He teaches mathematics at Hillsboro High School in Hillsboro, Oregon, and his teaching assignment encompasses students of all ability levels, including ESL. Jim believes that graphing calculators offer the best opportunity for large numbers of students to experience "hands-on" applications of technology. He favors learning activities where students are actively engaged in discovery. "Math is the study of patterns, but to really understand it you have to see it happen."

Jim likes e-mail, and he tries to answer all correspondence. He can be reached at **spechtj@hsd.k12.or.us** and **specht@teleport.com**.

INTRODUCTION

"What do you remember from your algebra class?" Pose this question to parents at your next open house. Watch their faces. Watch their eyes. There will probably be a few nervous laughs, but it's really a rhetorical question that requires no answer. Unless they have practiced algebra, what people remember about algebra is how it made them feel. Those who understood it probably felt empowered and continued their studies in mathematics. Those who did not probably exited their high school's math program at the earliest opportunity in what was, effectively, a career decision. What if today's technology had been available then? Would it have affected what people now remember from their algebra classes? If those classes had been accompanied by effective instruction in the use of that technology, the answer would probably have to be yes.

The National Council of Teachers of Mathematics urges the integration of technology in secondary mathematics instruction. There are four points to that vision.

✔ Appropriate calculators should be available to all students at all times.

✔ A computer should be available in every classroom for demonstration purposes.

✔ Every student shall have access to a computer for individual and group work.

✔ Students should learn to use the computer as a tool for processing information and performing calculations to investigate and solve problems.

As advances are made in the power of programmable graphing calculators, the lines between calculators and computers have become more and more blurred. These calculators can now assume many of the tasks that were once the sole domain of computers. As a result, the potential for the active integration of technology into regular math programs has moved dramatically closer to reality. Let's not confine technology's use to advanced levels of mathematics, where only a small number of students will have the opportunity to experience it. Rather, let's introduce students to graphing calculators while the majority of students are still participating in math programs.

The goal of *More Than Graphs* is to provide beginning algebra students with meaningful experiences in which they can use graphing calculators. The activities in this book are meant to be duplicated for classroom use. The lessons were written for the TI-73, TI-82, TI-83, and TI-83 Plus graphing calculators, manufactured by Texas Instruments. Not all of the activities have been modified to accommodate each calculator. My preference is for the TI-83, and that is the calculator featured in this book.

Helpful Hints

✔ An overhead calculator with a view screen is helpful for showing keystrokes, but a transparency of the diagram inside the calculator owner's manual is a good alternative.

✔ When possible, ask students to work together in groups so that they can assist one another. Let students share their discoveries and explorations. Students enjoy being partners in learning.

✔ Inputting programs can be tedious. To download a program from the CD, you need the cable to link calculator to computer and TI Connect™ software (available from education.ti.com). Check the instructions for your calculator. In general, you will open the More Than Graphs CD so you have a window on your desktop showing its contents. Connect the computer to the calculator and turn it on. Start TI Connect, choose the correct calculator from the **Connection** menu (Mac) or open the Device Explorer (Windows), then drag and drop the program from the CD window onto the window that represents the calculator. The program is now on the calculator. Use the linking cables to share the program with other calculators; data can also be shared. A word of warning: The first few times your class tries to link may be rather chaotic. The most common problem is that students have not pushed the linking connector firmly into their calculators. Don't be discouraged, before long students will become very skilled at sharing programs and data.

✔ If possible, allow students to take the school calculators home overnight for individual exploration. The impact of allowing students to show parents their new calculator skills can be dramatic.

✔ Don't be surprised if very soon some of your students become more proficient on the calculator than you are.

✔ Have an extra set or two of AAA batteries handy. If using a TI-82, save programs on a computer or to an empty calculator before replacing batteries. This will help you and your students avoid a memory loss.

✔ The screens of the different calculator models are not the same size. WINDOW settings for one may create a different-looking graph on another calculator. (See the *Circles and Eggs* activity for a detailed discussion of screen sizes and windows.)

✔ The calculator models do not share the same commands. Although many of the commands are similar, they don't always work in the same way.

✔ Contact Texas Instruments at ti-cares@ti.com for technical assistance.

I believe that math is best learned when it is seen and experienced, so I have tried in this book to include many activities in which students can see the mathematics they are doing. The lessons do not need to be taught in a specific order, but some activities work best when they follow one or more of the other activities.

I have used these lessons in classes where students were using a variety of graphing calculators. Students did one lesson each week on a day designated as TI-Tuesday. On this day, students left their math books in their lockers and we did calculator explorations. Although the students definitely learned at different speeds, and students who owned a graphing calculator had a definite advantage over those who used them only in class, all students rated their work with the graphing calculators the most meaningful of all their math learning experiences over the year.

I hope the calculators and these lessons work as well for you and your students.

Jim Specht

Circles and Eggs

The Visible Effects of Changing Windows

Setting the Stage

The equation for a circle is $x^2 + y^2 = r^2$.
If you graph all the possible solutions to
the equation $x^2 + y^2 = 4$, you will create
a circle with a radius of 2 because 4 represents the radius squared and $2^2 = 4$.
The center will be at the origin, $(0, 0)$.
The WINDOW values you choose will
affect the shape of this circle on the
calculator screen.

The Activity

The TI calculators can only graph functions. An equation
represents a function when each *x*-value matches up with exactly one *y*-value. Because of
this it is necessary to graph two equations in order to graph the circle.

$Y1 = \sqrt{(4 - x^2)}$ This equation will graph the top half of the circle.
$Y2 = {}^-\sqrt{(4 - x^2)}$ This equation will graph the bottom half of the circle.

Press (ZOOM) (6), and you will see the curve in a window
where the *x*-values are between $^+10$ and $^-10$, and the *y*-values
are between $^+10$ and $^-10$. This is referred to by some
mathematicians as the Dolciani window. It is named after an
author of algebra texts who displayed most of her graphing
exercises in this frame.

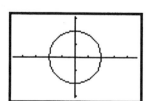

The circle in this window appears to be egg-shaped, or something nearer to a rugby ball
than a circle. The screen is divided into small units called *pixels*. The rectangular screen will
cause distortion unless you adjust the WINDOW values. You can see the *x*- and *y*-values of
each pixel on the circle by pressing (TRACE) followed by the right and left arrow keys. Each
time you push an arrow key, the cursor moves one pixel in the *x*-direction. Press (TRACE) and
use the arrow keys to see the approximate values for each pixel on the circle.

If you press (ZOOM) (4) (or (ZOOM) (8) on the TI-73), the circle will look more like a circle.
The origin is still in the center, just as before, but the window now
has a different frame. (Press (WINDOW) to see the new dimensions.)
Use (TRACE) to find out how big the pixels are in this window.
These *x*-values will seem much friendlier. This is why a window
like this is often called a **friendly window**. (The dimensions of
the friendly window will vary according to the particular calculator you are using.)

There are other ways to change the window to make it work better, depending on the function you want to graph. An integer window can be built by multiplying each setting in the friendly window by 10. Now each pixel will be worth one unit. The TI-73, TI-82, TI-83, and TI-83 Plus can actually do this calculation within the WINDOW screen. When entering Xmax, for example, you could enter 9.4 · 10. The TI-82, TI-83, and TI-83 Plus also have an option (ZOOM 8) that creates an integer window automatically. (This is ZOOM 0 on the TI-73.)The integer window is very friendly because when you trace, you will get only whole-number values for x. Perpendicular lines, polygons, and other geometric figures drawn using a friendly decimal window or a very friendly integer window will appear very true to those drawn on graph paper without the distortion caused by using the standard settings with the rectangular screen.

If you have a graph and want a close-up view of part of it, you can use ZOOM 2, which zooms in. First position the cursor on the place that you want to be the center of the new graph. Then press ZOOM 2 ENTER. To zoom out and get the bird's-eye view, use ZOOM 3. These two zooms move you closer in or further out by changing the Xmax, Xmin, Ymax, and Ymin. The scale is not changed. The WINDOW values change by factors of 4 or 0.25, but the ZOOM factor settings can be changed by selecting MEMORY (Set Factors) from the ZOOM menu.

A useful way to zoom, which gives you a lot of control, is ZBox. Press ZOOM 1. Now move the cursor to one corner of the area you want to enlarge and press ENTER. Move the cursor to the opposite corner of the area you want to enlarge and press ENTER again, and voila! You may want to press WINDOW to see the new WINDOW settings you designed.

For WINDOW readings, a TI-73 will also give a ΔX-value. That is the value that the calculator has assigned to each x-pixel when it uses the current Xmin and Xmax values.

Practice Problems

Each picture below is generated by the equation $x^2 + y^2 = 9$.
Graph the equation by entering Y1 = $\sqrt{(9-x^2)}$ and Y2 = $^-\sqrt{(9-x^2)}$. Find the WINDOW settings needed to show each picture of the equation.

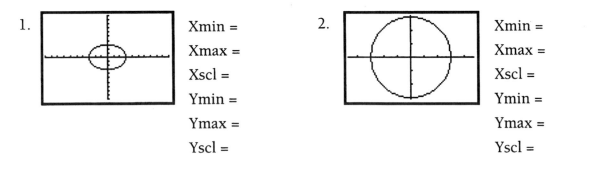

1.
Xmin =
Xmax =
Xscl =
Ymin =
Ymax =
Yscl =

2.
Xmin =
Xmax =
Xscl =
Ymin =
Ymax =
Yscl =

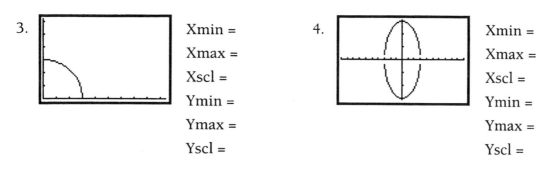

3. Xmin =
   Xmax =
   Xscl =
   Ymin =
   Ymax =
   Yscl =

4. Xmin =
   Xmax =
   Xscl =
   Ymin =
   Ymax =
   Yscl =

5. Sometimes when you graph a function it won't be there. This is because either you have turned off the function in Y= or the function is not visible within the WINDOW screen you have defined. For each function listed below, start with a friendly window defined by ⦅ZOOM⦆ ④ on the TI-82, TI-83, and TI-83 Plus, and ⦅ZOOM⦆ ⑧ on the TI-73. For the TI-81 use these settings: [⁻4.6, 4.7, 1, ⁻3.1, 3.2, 1]. Enter the function into Y= and press ⦅GRAPH⦆. Then zoom out until you "find" the function. (Don't forget to press ⦅ENTER⦆ after choosing Zoom Out.) TRACE on the function to help you determine good WINDOW values for viewing the graph. (Be prepared to defend your choices.) Enter these values into the WINDOW settings and graph the function again to verify that it is indeed a good window. Record your final WINDOW settings and write a sentence explaining why you like this particular window.
   a. $y = 2x - 15$
   b. $y = 3x^2 - 2x + 8$
   c. $y = {}^{-}0.5x^2 + 12x - 15$

Extension Problems

1. a. Based on what you learned about the equation of a circle, describe what the graph of the equation $y = \sqrt{100 - x^2}$ should look like.
   b. Graph this equation using ⦅ZOOM⦆ ⑥. Now press ⦅ZOOM⦆ ⑤. Describe what happens.
   c. Look at the WINDOW values. Which values have changed?
   d. What happens when you press ⦅ZOOM⦆ ④ (or ⦅ZOOM⦆ ⑧ on the TI-73)?
   e. Name a friendly window that pictures the whole graph.
   f. Graph the equation again using ⦅ZOOM⦆ ⑥. Then press ⦅ZOOM⦆ ⑧ (⦅ZOOM⦆ ⓪ on the TI-73) and press ⦅ENTER⦆. Describe what happens.
   g. Look at the WINDOW values. Which values have changed?
   h. Write a paragraph comparing and contrasting the effects of the different ZOOM commands.

2. a. Graph the two equations: $y = 5x + 10$ and $y = {}^{-}0.2x - 5.6$ using ⦅ZOOM⦆ ⑥. These two lines are actually perpendicular. Experiment with different zooms and windows and see what happens. Name two different windows that picture the perpendicularity of these lines.

b. Find a window that will allow you to trace to find the point of intersection. Check that this is really the point of intersection by substituting the values into each of the given equations.

c. Write an explanation for a friend who was absent from class, describing what you did in this problem and what your results were.

More Than Graphs, Revised Edition • ©2004 Key Curriculum Press

Circles and Eggs

Objective: To study viewing and tracing changes effected by different WINDOW settings and ZOOMs

Materials needed: TI-73, TI-82, TI-83, or TI-83 Plus graphing calculator

Appropriate level: Algebra and possibly pre-algebra

Time involved: One class period

Preparation: Familiarity with Cartesian coordinates

WINDOW settings are a persistent problem for some people. The settings you choose actually control two aspects of graphing functions—the viewing area and the TRACE values. After entering an equation and pressing (GRAPH), there is often a moment of panic when the student assumes, "Oh, no! It's gone." Actually, what has usually happened is one of two things—the domain and range of the graph are outside the WINDOW dimensions, or the equation is set to be inactive. The WINDOW settings will also affect what values show on the screen when you trace a function.

When initially graphing an equation, use settings where there is a high probability of finding data or values. (ZOOM) (6) is usually a good place to start. Next, make adjustments for a friendly window, particularly if you want friendly tracing values or you want to eliminate the distortion caused by using standard settings on a rectangular screen. In order for a window to be friendly, the *x*-range must be a factor of the number of horizontal pixels and the *y*-range must be a factor of the number of vertical pixels. The screen dimensions on the TI-73, TI-82, TI-83, and TI-83 Plus are all 94×62 pixels.

Therefore, in order for the TRACE numbers to be "friendly," the difference $Xmax - Xmin$ must always be a factor of 94 and the difference $Ymax - Ymin$ must be a factor of 62. Thus, each of the following windows will be "friendly."

TI-82

Xmin = −4.7	Xmin = −14.1	Xmin = 0
Xmax = 4.7	Xmax = 14.1	Xmax = 47
Xscl = 1	Xscl = 5	Xscl = 5
Ymin = −3.1	Ymin = −9.3	Ymin = 0
Ymax = 3.1	Ymax = 9.3	Ymax = 31
Yscl = 1	Yscl = 5	Yscl = 5

To make an equation active, just press (Y=) and use the cursor to highlight the = sign. Then press (ENTER). When the = sign is darkened, that means that the equation will be plotted.

Solutions

Practice Problems

1. ZStandard [⁻10, 10, 1, ⁻10, 10, 1]
2. ZDecimal [⁻4.7, 4.7, 1, ⁻3.1, 3.1, 1]
3. [0, 9.4, 1, 0, 6.2, 1]
4. [⁻9.4, 9.4, 1, ⁻3.1, 3.1, 1]
5. a, b, and c. Answers will vary.

Extension Problems

1. a. The graph of the equation is a semicircle centered at the origin with radius of 10.
   b. In (ZOOM) (6), you get the top of a football; (ZOOM) (5) makes it look more circlelike.
   c. The Xmin changes from ⁻10 to ⁻15.16129, and the Xmax changes from 10 to 15.16129.
   d. The window gets so small that you can't see the graph of the semicircle. (On a TI-73, you see only the first quadrant.)
   e. (ZOOM) (5) [⁻15.16129, 15.16129, 1, ⁻10, 10]
   f. (ZOOM) (8) gives a large window, with the semicircle appearing to be very small.
   g. All the WINDOW values have changed. The new window is [⁻47, 47, 10, ⁻31, 31].
   h. Your students' paragraphs should summarize their results from the first seven problems.
2. a. ZSquare and ZInteger both picture the perpendicularity.
   b. Using ZInteger, you can trace and find that the point of intersection is (⁻3, ⁻5). This is (ZOOM) (0) on the TI-73 and (ZOOM) (8) on the TI-82, TI-83, and TI-83 Plus.
   c. Answers will vary.

More Than Graphs, Revised Edition • ©2004 Key Curriculum Press

Absolutely!
Graphing Absolute Value Functions

Setting the Stage

Aage, Beth, Carey, and Donisha all live on the same east-west subway route, which they ride when going to school. One way to show where they live relative to the school is by using a diagram like the one below.

| Aage | Beth | | School | Carey | Donisha |

You can use the absolute value function to find the distance between the subway stops for any pair of students. How far is it from Donisha's subway stop to Beth's subway stop? To find the distance between two points on a line, you subtract one value from the other. So the distance would be $|{-8.4} - 9.8|$ or $|9.8 - {-8.4}|$.

The Activity

The absolute value of a number is the distance on a number line from the number to zero. Since distance is always positive, so is the absolute value of any number. As an example, the absolute value of $^-7$ is 7. This is written $|{-7}| = 7$. On your graphing calculator, [ABS] finds absolute value. To enter [ABS] press (MATH), select NUM, and press (ENTER). Try using the absolute value function to find the distance between Donisha's subway stop and Beth's subway stop.

You can also use [ABS] to graph absolute value functions. You may be surprised by the results. Graph $Y1 = abs\ x$.

Press (TRACE) and use the right and left arrows to explore the graph. Complete the following statements in terms of x:

If $x \leq 0$, then $|x| =$ _____.
If $x > 0$, then $|x| =$ _____.

The two sentences you just completed give the definition of absolute value. In the problems you will have a chance to play with and explore the absolute value function.

Practice Problems

1. In Urban Geography class, Aage, Beth, Carey, and Donisha have to make a chart of the distances between their subway stops. Complete the chart using the absolute value function to find each distance.

	Donisha	Carey	Beth
Aage			
Beth			
Carey			

2. Graph Y1= x^2 – 3. Now turn off Y1 and graph Y2 = abs (x^2 – 3). Describe what happens, and make a sketch on the blank screen.

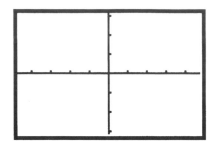

3. Graph Y1 = x^3. Now turn off Y1 and graph Y2 = abs x^3. Describe what happens, and make a sketch on the blank screen.

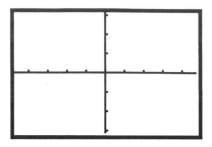

4. Graph Y1 = $^-x^2$. Predict what you think will happen if you graph Y2 = abs ($^-x^2$). Turn off Y1 and graph Y2. Describe what happens, and make a sketch on the blank screen.

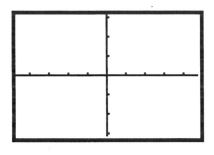

5. Graph Y1 = x. Now turn off Y1 and graph Y2 = abs x. Describe what happens, and make a sketch on the blank screen.

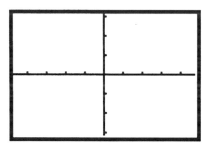

6. Graph Y1 = abs (x + 2), and make a sketch on the blank screen. How does this graph compare to the second graph in Problem 5?

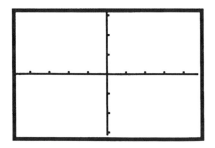

7. Predict what the graph of Y1 = abs (x – 2) will look like. Graph it and make a sketch on the blank screen.

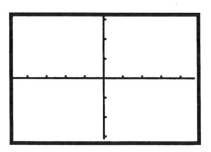

More Than Graphs, Revised Edition • ©2004 Key Curriculum Press

8. Write a letter to a friend who was absent from school when you did this activity. Explain what effect abs has on the graph of a function. What do all graphed absolute value functions seem to have in common?

Extension Problems

1. The graph of the absolute value of a function is always positive. What would you expect to happen if you were to graph the opposite of the absolute value of a function? Graph Y1 = ⁻abs x. Describe how this graph is related to the graph of y = abs x. Try this with several other functions in the Practice Problems.

2. Look at the graphs made by graphing the equations y = |x + 1| and y = ⁻abs (x − 1). Adding or subtracting a number from these functions will shift the graphs left or right. Graph these functions on the same screen.
   Y1 = abs (x + 1) − 2
   Y2 = ⁻abs (x − 1) + 2
   What effect does the negative sign in front of the abs in the second equation have on the graph?
   Press (ZOOM) (4) ((ZOOM) (8) on the TI-73), and draw a picture of the shape you see on the screen.

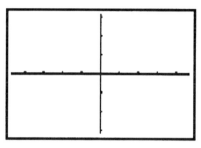

   a. Name the shape that is bounded by the two functions.
   b. What is the area of this shape?
   c. Approximately what percentage of the screen is enclosed by this shape?
   d. If the Xmin, Ymin, Xmax, and Ymax were doubled, how would that affect the percentage of the area enclosed by the shape?

Absolutely!

Objective:	To use the calculator to explore the absolute value function
Materials needed:	TI-73, TI-82, TI-83, or TI-83 Plus graphing calculator
Appropriate level:	Algebra and pre-algebra
Time involved:	One hour or class period
Preparation:	None

Absolutely! explores a concept in algebra that many students don't understand. The calculator is a powerful tool for demystifying the concept of absolute value by giving students an opportunity to visualize what the absolute value function does to a graph. The first part of the activity involves looking at the absolute value of a number as a solution to a distance problem. In these problems you may need to remind your students to use parentheses, which can lead to a review of order of operations. The second part of the activity involves graphing functions involving absolute value and making generalizations from the graphs.

This activity is a nice follow-up to *Circles and Eggs*, because the Extension involves finding friendly windows.

Solutions

Practice Problems

1.

	Donisha	Carey	Beth
Aage	25	18.4	6.8
Beth	18.2	11.6	
Carey	6.6		11.6

2. [⁻4.7, 4.7, 1, ⁻3.1, 3.1, 1]

$y = x^2 - 3$

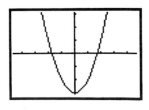

$y = |x^2 - 3|$

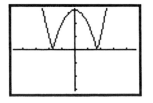

 More Than Graphs, Revised Edition • ©2004 Key Curriculum Press

3. $y = x^3$

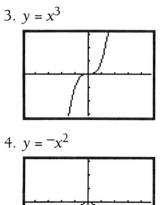

$y = |x^3|$

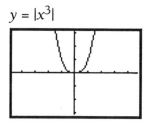

4. $y = {}^-x^2$

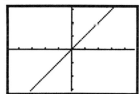

$y = |{}^-x^2|$

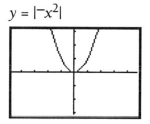

5. $y = x$

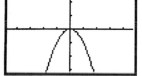

$y = |x|$

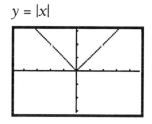

6. $y = |x + 2|$

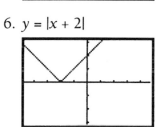

7. $y = |x - 2|$

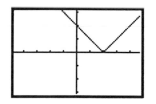

8. Answers will vary. In the problems above, the absolute value graphs have only positive y-values.

Extension Problems

1. If you graph the opposite of an absolute value function, the y-values are all negative.
2. a. The shape is a rectangle.
   b. The area is 6. You can find this using the distance formula, or by dividing the rectangle into small right triangles such as the one with vertices $(0, 0)$, $(1, 0)$, and $(0, {}^{-}1)$. Each of these triangles has an area of $\frac{1}{2}$, and there are 12 of them, so the total area is 6.
   c. The shape fills approximately 10% of the screen. The area of the screen is $9.4 \cdot 6.2 = 58.28$, and $\frac{6}{58.28} = 0.10295$.
   d. WINDOW dimensions can be doubled by multiplying each max and min by 2 in the WINDOW screen. If they are doubled, the percentage of area taken up by the shape on the screen is divided by 4.

What's My Line?

Finding an Equation of a Line Given Three Collinear Points

Setting the Stage

One of the first postulates, or laws, in geometry is that two points determine a unique line. This means that any time you have two points, there is one and only one line that passes through

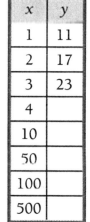

them. Ordered pairs correspond to points in the Cartesian plane. If you have two sets of ordered pairs, you can find the equation of the line that passes through them. Once you have an equation, you can use that equation to find coordinates for any other point on the line. Linear equations can be used to model many real-life situations.

In this activity you will be given the coordinates of three collinear points. You will enter this information into your calculator, and your calculator will figure out the equation of the line that passes through these points. Then you will be given some x-values, and you will find the corresponding y-value for each x-value.

x	y
1	11
2	17
3	23
4	
10	
50	
100	
500	

The Activity

Follow the steps in this example to find the equation of the line that passes through the three given points. Then find the missing y-values.

Step 1: Press STAT and choose Edit (press LIST on the TI-73) to enter the first three x-values in L1 and the y-values in L2. (If there are numbers already in a list, use the up arrow key to move the cursor so that it highlights the name of the list you want to clear. Press CLEAR ENTER, and the list entries will disappear.)

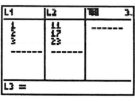

Step 2: Enter appropriate values for Xmin, Xmax, Ymin, and Ymax after pressing WINDOW. Be sure your screen will show all four quadrants. A window for this example might be [⁻10, 10, 1, ⁻30, 30, 10, 1]. On the TI-73, TI-83, and TI-83 Plus, the Xres setting will tell how often the x-values are recalculated. The default is Xres=1, where the function is evaluated at every pixel. The TI-73 will also have a ΔX-value, indicating the x-value that the calculator has assigned to each pixel.

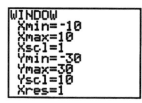

Step 3: Press $\boxed{\text{2nd}}$ [$\boxed{\text{STAT PLOT}}$] ($\boxed{\text{2nd}}$ [PLOT] on the TI-73), choose the settings as shown below, and press $\boxed{\text{GRAPH}}$ to display the points.

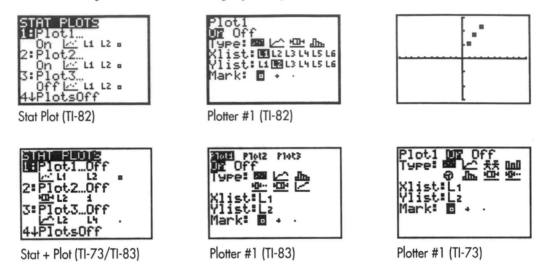

Stat Plot (TI-82)   Plotter #1 (TI-82)

Stat + Plot (TI-73/TI-83)   Plotter #1 (TI-83)   Plotter #1 (TI-73)

Step 4: To find the equation of the line, press $\boxed{\text{STAT}}$ CALC ($\boxed{\text{2nd}}$ $\boxed{\text{STAT}}$ CALC on the TI-73). Choose LinReg($ax+b$) to do a linear regression, which will calculate the equation of the line passing through the points whose coordinates are stored in L1 and L2. (The calculator may also show an r-value, which will be studied in a later activity.)

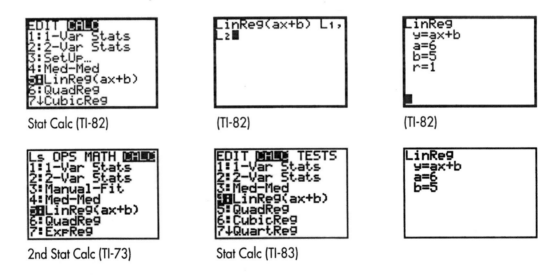

Stat Calc (TI-82)   (TI-82)   (TI-82)

2nd Stat Calc (TI-73)   Stat Calc (TI-83)

Step 5: Press $\boxed{\text{Y=}}$ and enter this equation into Y1.   Step 6: Press $\boxed{\text{GRAPH}}$ to graph the line.

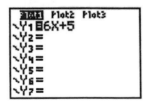 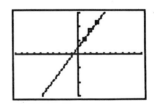

Step 7: Find the other *y*-values and complete the table. You can do this by entering the numbers directly each time, or you can press [2nd] [ENTRY] and use the arrow keys and [DEL] (delete) and/or [2nd] [INS] (insert) to edit the expression.

```
6*4+5
          29
```

```
6*4+5
          29
6*10+5
          65
```

```
              65
6*50+5
            305
6*100+5
            605
6*500+5
           3005
```

...

x	y
1	11
2	17
3	23
4	29
10	65
50	305
100	605
500	3005

Practice Problems

Plot the given points in each table and find the equation of the line that contains the points. Then use the equation to find the missing *y*-values.

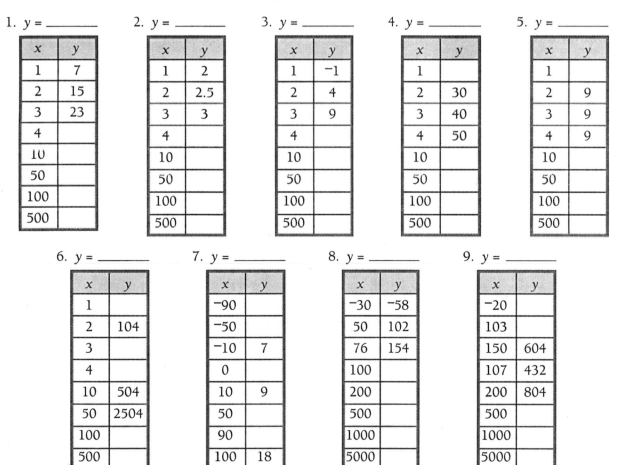

1. y = _____

x	y
1	7
2	15
3	23
4	
10	
50	
100	
500	

2. y = _____

x	y
1	2
2	2.5
3	3
4	
10	
50	
100	
500	

3. y = _____

x	y
1	−1
2	4
3	9
4	
10	
50	
100	
500	

4. y = _____

x	y
1	
2	30
3	40
4	50
10	
50	
100	
500	

5. y = _____

x	y
1	
2	9
3	9
4	9
10	
50	
100	
500	

6. y = _____

x	y
1	
2	104
3	
4	
10	504
50	2504
100	
500	

7. y = _____

x	y
−90	
−50	
−10	7
0	
10	9
50	
90	
100	18

8. y = _____

x	y
−30	−58
50	102
76	154
100	
200	
500	
1000	
5000	

9. y = _____

x	y
−20	
103	
150	604
107	432
200	804
500	
1000	
5000	

Extension Problems

1. After you plot the points and graph the equation, experiment with [TRACE] and [ZOOM] to look for x- and y-values. (The up and down arrows will move the cursor between the plotted points and the graphed line. If you see P1 in the upper right-hand corner of the screen, you are tracing the points. If a 1 is there on the TI-82, or the equation of the function on the TI-73, TI-83, or TI-83 Plus, you are tracing the function.) What effects do different ZOOMs have on the TRACE values? Try ZDecimal, ZSquare, ZStandard, and ZInteger. Explain what effect each of these ZOOMs has on the WINDOW settings and the TRACE values.

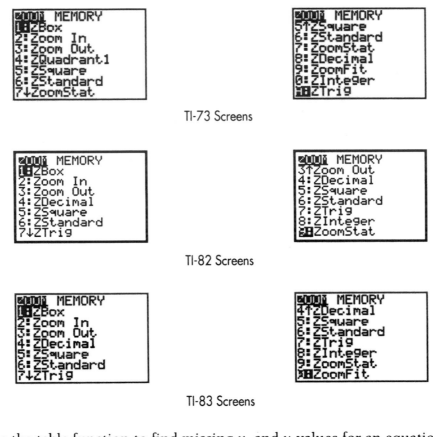

TI-73 Screens

TI-82 Screens

TI-83 Screens

2. You can use the table function to find missing x- and y-values for an equation.

   Enter an equation from one of the Practice Problems in Y1.

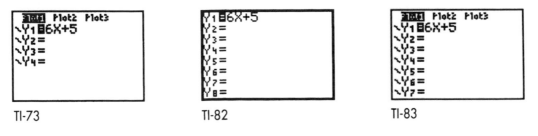

TI-73   TI-82   TI-83

More Than Graphs, Revised Edition • ©2004 Key Curriculum Press

Press ⌜ 2nd ⌝ [TABLE] (above ⌜GRAPH⌝) to see a table of values for *x* and *y*.

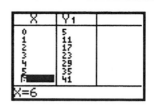

Press ⌜ 2nd ⌝ [TblSet] (above ⌜WINDOW⌝) to experiment with different values for TblMin and ΔTbl. See what effect they have on the table entries.

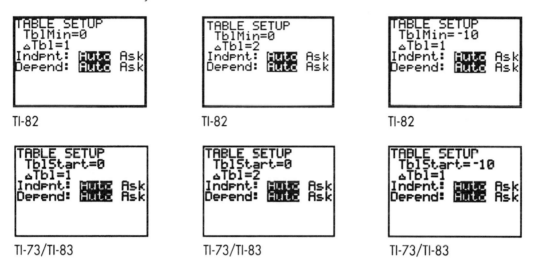

TI-82   TI-82   TI-82

TI-73/TI-83   TI-73/TI-83   TI-73/TI-83

Experiment with Indpnt: Auto Ask and Depend: Auto Ask in the TABLE SETUP window.

3. Another way to find a *y*-value for a given *x*-value is by using the Y-VARS menu. Be sure you have an equation in Y₁.

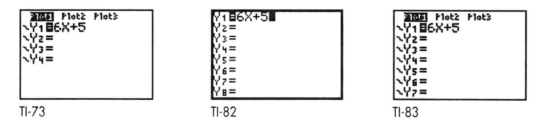

TI-73   TI-82   TI-83

Find the value of *y* when *x* = 42. Press [2nd] [VARS] to get the Y-VARS menu on the
TI-83 and TI-83 Plus; press [2nd] [VARS] on the TI-73; and press [2nd] [Y-VARS] on
the TI-82.

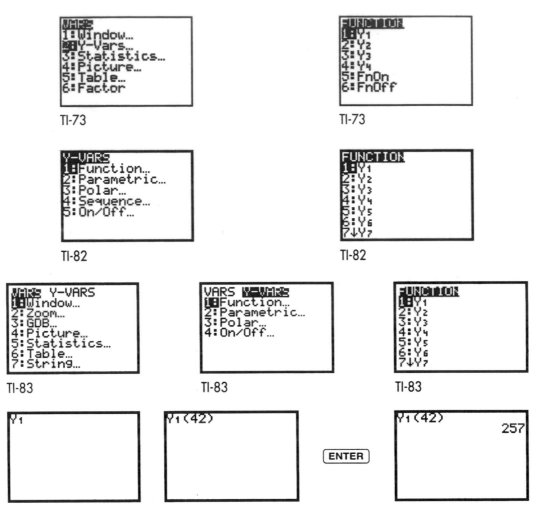

By pressing [2nd] [ENTRY], and using the arrow keys and [DEL] or [2nd] [INS], you can
change 42 to any *x*-value and find the corresponding *y*-value.

What's My Line?

Objective:	To use the linear regression function to find the equation of a line given three collinear points
Materials needed:	TI-73, TI-82, TI-83, or TI-83 Plus graphing calculator
Appropriate level:	Algebra and pre-algebra
Time involved:	One hour or class period
Preparation:	Some familiarity with points, lines, and substitution

This activity introduces students to variables, equations, and graphing, which are all essential concepts in the study of algebra. It also shows students how the same problem can be solved using a variety of calculator techniques. Encourage students to experiment. They may even invent their own methods for completing the tables. Let students work together and share their solutions.

Although students use the linear regression calculator function to find the equation of a line,
they are not really finding a line of best fit because they are working with given collinear points rather than experimental data points. Consequently the correlation coefficient, r, will always be 1 or $^-1$. Students will learn more about the r-value in a later activity.

Students enjoy this activity and they begin to understand the real power of a graphing calculator—that it isn't just a machine for number crunching.

Solutions

Practice Problems

1. $y = 8x - 1$ 31, 79, 399, 799, 3999
2. $y = 0.5x + 1.5$ 3.5, 6.5, 26.6, 51.5, 251.5
3. $y = 5x - 6$ 14, 44, 244, 494, 2494
4. $y = 10x + 10$ 20, 110, 510, 1010, 5010
5. $y = 9$ 9, 9, 9, 9, 9
6. $y = 50x + 4$ 54; 154; 5004; 25,004
7. $y = 0.1x + 8$ $^-1$, 3, 8, 13, 17
8. $y = 2x + 2$ 202; 402; 1002; 2002; 10,002
9. $y = 4x + 4$ $^-76$; 416; 2004; 4004; 20,004

Extension Problems

Answers will vary.

How Similar Are We?

Making Predictions Based on Data

Setting the Stage

"You're the image of your father!" "You're the image of your mother!" Have you ever heard these words? Do you think they're true? How much more similar are two people if they are related than if they are friends or acquaintances? In this activity, you will study this question by collecting a variety of measurements for yourself and a partner. For a partner, you may choose to use a parent, a brother or sister, or a friend. You will input these measurements into your calculator in order to find a line of best fit, which you will compare to the lines generated by your classmates. You will also use your line of best fit to make a prediction about other body measurements that you did not measure originally. Then you will check your predictions to see how accurate they were.

The Activity

Collecting the Data

Fill in the table with your measurements and those of your partner. Indicate who your partner is so that your data can be compared to that of your classmates. You must also decide whether to measure using inches or centimeters.

Partner's name: _____

Partner's relationship to you: _____

Body Measurement	Your Measurement	Your Partner's Measurement	Ratio: Your Measurement / Partner's Measurement	Ratio as a Decimal
Length of foot				
Height				
Width of shoulders				
Length of collar				
Circumference of thumb				
Distance from tip of nose to tip of index finger with arm outstretched				

Practice Problems

Analyzing the Data

1. Enter your measurements into L1 and your partner's measurements into L2. Choose appropriate WINDOW values, and plot the data in a scatter plot.
2. For each measurement, write the ratio comparing your measurement to your partner's measurement. Rewrite this ratio as a decimal. (You can do this in list L3 by moving your cursor up until it is on L3 and entering L2/L1.) Compare your results with those of other members of your group.
3. Use a LinReg function in the STAT CALC menu to find a function that relates your measurements to your partner's measurements. (Be sure to make note of the r-value. On the TI-82, the r-value is a default setting and always shows when doing linear regression; on the TI-83 and TI-73, it is an option that must be requested to be seen. The easiest way to do this is to access the CATALOG and go to DiagnosticsOn. The CATALOG feature is accessed by pressing [2nd] [CATALOG] on both the TI-83 and the TI-73.) Enter this function into Y1, and graph the line over the points.

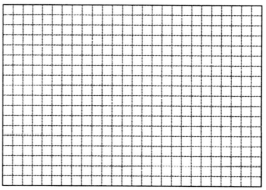

4. The r-value is a measure of how well the line fits the data. It is called the *correlation coefficient*, and is always between $^-1$ and 1. The closer r is to 1 or $^-1$, the better the line fits the data. How well do you think the line fits your data?
5. Name three other body parts and measure the length of each. Use your function to predict the corresponding measurements for your partner.

Body Part Measured	Your Measurement	Your Partner's Measurement (Predicted)	Your Partner's Measurement (Actual)

6. Write a few sentences explaining how well you think your model (function) works.
7. Compare the ratios you found, your line of best fit, and your r-values with other members of your class. Is there less variation in the data generated by partners who are related than for partners who are not related? Discuss this with your group members or as a class and state your conclusions.

Extension Problems

Body measurements were often used in early measurement and construction. The *cubit* that Noah used to build the ark was the distance of his forearm, measured between elbow and wrist. In creating the original English system of measurement, the *foot* and the *hand* were standards of measurement meant to coincide with the measure of a king's foot and a king's hand. A *fathom* was the extreme distance between fingertips of both outstretched arms. You might call this a "wingspan." A *yard* was the distance from one fingertip to the center of the chest. Feet are still a common unit of measure in the United States today, and hands are often used to determine the height of horses.

1. It is said that a person's wingspan should be approximately the same as his or her height. Your wingspan is the distance from the tip of your middle finger on one hand to the tip of your middle finger on the other hand with your arms outstretched. Collect height and wingspan measurements from at least five classmates, including yourself. See how close these measurements are to each other by computing the ratio in the table. The closer this ratio is to 1, the more nearly equal the measurements are.

Student	Wingspan	Height	$\dfrac{\text{Wingspan}}{\text{Height}}$
Self			
1.			
2.			
3.			
4.			

2. A similar notion is that the length of a person's forearm is about the same as his or her foot size. Confirm or deny the accuracy of this by conducting your own experiment.

Student	Forearm Length	Shoe Length	$\dfrac{\text{Forearm Length}}{\text{Shoe Length}}$
Self			
1.			
2.			
3.			
4.			

How Similar Are We?

Objective: To make a prediction by evaluating measured data
Materials needed: TI-73, TI-82, TI-83, or TI-83 Plus graphing calculator
Appropriate level: Algebra and pre-algebra
Time involved: One hour or class period
Preparation: Bring a parent's measurements to class

This is an extension of *What's My Line?* but in this activity students use actual data, which they collect in class and at home. The process of analyzing the data is the same. Students will use the calculator to find a best-fit line from the data. They will then use the line to compare data from related and nonrelated partners. They will also use the line of best fit to make predictions.

The real purpose of using data collected from home is to extend the walls of the math classroom. Students will be communicating with parents and/or family members about the technology and math they are studying in school.

The best-fit line will have a y-intercept close to zero and a slope equal to the ratio of proportionality. You might encourage a class discussion as to what factors will have the most effect on slope—relation, age, same gender, etc.

Although the correlation coefficient, r, is a very complicated concept and difficult to simplify at this level, you can discuss the idea that the closer the r-value is to 1, the better the correlation. The r^2-value is an indication of the percent of points that lie within a narrow band relative to the best-fit line. The results with my students have yielded an r-value of 0.9 or higher in almost every case, regardless of the relationship of the partners. This leads to interesting discussions of how human beings are all essentially the same.

I have found it interesting to have some students use English units while others use metric. It is valuable for students to see how using different units changes the scale of their graphs, but leaves the shape and relationship intact.

Solutions

Practice Problems

Answers will vary.

Extension Problems

Answers will vary.

Fibonacci Sequences

Using the Calculator to Generate and Examine Sequences

Setting the Stage

Leonardo Pisano (1170–1250) was the first great mathematician of medieval Europe. He is also known as Leonardo of Pisa or by his nickname, Leonardo Fibonacci. His father's name was Bonacci, so Leonardo acquired the name "Filius Bonacci" or son of Bonacci—Fibonacci for short.

Fibonacci was educated in Africa and traveled extensively in Europe and Asia Minor. Fibonacci was famous because he knew and understood the entire body of mathematical knowlege, both current and ancient. This made him very important in the revival of interest in the mathematics of the ancients. At the time most people used Roman numerals, and they avoided zero because they did not understand it. Fibonacci was influential in spreading the system of Arabic numerals with 10 different symbols and a place-holder, to replace the awkward Roman numerals. This is the number system we use today. Fibonacci did a great deal of new work in the study of number theory, and introduced the notion of what are still called Fibonacci sequences.

The Activity

A **Fibonacci sequence** is determined by the first two terms which are called *seeds*. Each successive term of the sequence is the sum of the two previous terms. The classic sequence starts with the seeds 1 and 1. The next term is 2, followed by 3, followed by 5, ...

Write the first 20 terms of the Fibonacci sequence:

1, 1, 2, 3, 5, ___, ___, ___, ___, ___, ___, ___, ___, ___, ___, ___, ___, ___, ___, ___

The truly astonishing thing about Fibonacci sequences is that they appear in many seemingly unrelated areas, including the spiral arrangement on certain flowers and plants, and the Golden Section in architecture and geometry.

The program will ask you for the number of terms in the sequence and then generate the terms, which will be stored in L1. When the program is done, press [2nd] [L1] ([2nd] [STAT] and select L1 on the TI-73) and then press the right and left arrow keys to scroll through the list of terms.

TI-82/TI-83 Program

```
PROGRAM:FIB
Disp "HOW MANY TERMS?"
Input C
ClrHome
ClrList L1,L2,L3
Disp "SEED 1"
Input X
X→L1(1)
Disp "SEED 2"
Input Y
Y→L1(2)
Y→L2(1)
L1(1)+L1(2)→L2(2)
For(N,3,C,1)
L1(N-1)+L1(N-2)→L1(N)
L1(N)+L1(N-1)→L2(N)
End
Disp L1
```

TI-73 Program

```
PROGRAM:FIB
Disp "HOW MANY TERMS?"
Input C
ClrScreen
ClrAllLists
Disp "SEED 1"
Input X
X→L1(1)
Disp "SEED 2"
Input Y
Y→L1(2)
Y→L2(1)
L1(1)+L1(2)→L2(2)
For(N,3,C,1)
L1(N-1)+L1(N-2)→L1(N)
L1(N)+L1(N-1)→L2(N)
End
Disp L1
Disp "(ENTER TWICE TO"
Disp "START AGAIN.)"
Pause
```

Practice Problems

Use your calculator, when necessary, to fill in the missing terms.

1. Use the program to find the first 20 terms of Fibonacci sequences using the given seeds.
   - a. 2, 4
   - b. 1, 3
   - c. 1, 5
   - d. you choose
2. The Golden Ratio

Run the program and use 1 and 1 as the two seed values.

Press ⎡ STAT ⎤ EDIT (⎡ LIST ⎤ on the TI-73) and look at the sequence of numbers in L1 and L2. Each term of the Fibonacci sequence should be in list L1, and the term that follows it should be in L2. List L1 should end with 6765 and L2 should end with 10946.

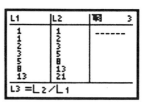

Now you are ready to discover something interesting that happens with the ratios of successive terms. Enter the formula L2/L1 in L3 so that L3 will show the ratio of each term of the Fibonacci sequence to the term that precedes it.

Scroll down list L3 and see what happens to the ratios. Do you notice that the ratios seem to be getting closer to a certain value as the sequence progresses?

What is that value? _____

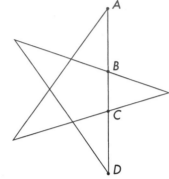

This ratio has been well-known since the days of the ancient Greeks, and it is often referred to as the Golden Ratio. You can find an example of this ratio in a pentagram.

$AC/BC = BD/CD = AD/BD =$ the Golden Ratio

Extension Problems

1. The sequence you worked with in Practice Problem 2 is the sequence that is known as the Fibonacci sequence. However, any sequence that follows the rule of adding successive terms to generate the next term is also called a Fibonacci sequence. Do some experimenting and see what happens to the ratio defined in Problem 2 if you choose other seed values. Try different pairs of positive numbers, negative numbers, and one positive and one negative number. Does the ratio still approach the same number in the long run? What happens if your seed values are fractions? Write a summary describing how you explored this problem and what your results were.

2. Solve these Fibonacci puzzles. You might want to use guess-and-check or an algebraic method for some of them.

   a. 2, 4, 6, 10, 16, ___, ___, ___, 110, . . .
   b. 3, 1, 4, 5, 9, 14, ___, ___, ___, 97, . . .
   c. 3, 7, ___, ___, ___, ___, 71, . . .
   d. 1, 5, ___, ___, ___, ___, ___, 73, . . .
   e. 6, ___, 14, ___, ___, ___, ___, ___, 246, . . .
   f. 2, ___, 10, ___, ___, ___, ___, ___, 194, . . .
   g. 6, ___, ___, 12, ___, ___, ___, 87, . . .
   h. 1, ___, ___, ___, 14, ___, ___, 60, . . .
   i. 3, ___, ___, ___, 30, ___, ___, 128, . . .
   j. 6, ___, ___, ___, ___, ___, ___, ___, 183, . . .
   k. 5, ___, ___, 12, ___, ___, 53, . . .
   l. Create a puzzle of your own and ask a friend to solve it.

Fibonacci Sequences

Objective: To study Fibonacci sequences and the ratio between successive terms
Materials needed: TI-73, TI-82, TI-83, or TI-83 Plus graphing calculator
Appropriate level: Algebra and pre-algebra
Time involved: One hour or class period
Preparation: Some basic understanding about generating sequences

In this activity students use a program to generate Fibonacci sequences. The terms are stored in L1, which allows students to examine the terms either by looking at the list in the STAT menu or by displaying the list on the Home screen. In the Practice Problems, students explore what happens to the ratio of successive terms in the long run. In the first Extension problem, students are encouraged to explore what happens when they choose various kinds of numbers for the seed values.

If students have done the Shape Shifter activity, they could revisit it at this time and draw a five-pointed star. They could then trace to find the coordinates of the points shown in the figure, and using the distance formula (Editing Pythagoras activity), they could verify that the ratios given are indeed the Golden Ratio.

The Fibonacci puzzles in the extension can be very challenging. One way to solve Fibonacci sequences is by using problem-solving strategies like guess and check and/or working backward. This becomes more difficult when several consecutive terms are absent and one of the first two is among them. Algebra can help here. Consider the sequence $1, \ldots, 15, \ldots$ If you let the second term be x, the sequence becomes: $1, x, 1 + x, x + (1 + x), (1 + x) + (x + (1 + x)), \ldots$. The fifth term equals $3 + 3x$. In the first problem, the fifth term is also 15. Since they're the same problem, $3 + 3x = 15$, then x must equal 4. Knowing that the second term is 4 allows you to go back and fill in every blank.

Solutions

Practice Problems

1. a. {2, 4, 6, 10, 16, 26, 42, 68, 110, 178, 288, 466, 754, 1220, 1974, 3194, 5168, 8362, 15350, 21892}
   b. {1, 3, 4, 7, 11, 18, 29, 47, 76, 123, 199, 322, 521, 843, 1364, 2207, 3571, 5778, 9349, 15127}
   c. {1, 5, 6, 11, 17, 28, 45, 73, 118, 191, 309, 500, 809, 1309, 2118, 3427, 5545, 8972, 14517, 23489}
   d. Answers will vary.
2. As the terms get larger, the ratio becomes 1.618 . . . , the Golden Ratio.

Extension Problems

1. Answers will vary.
2. a. 2, 4, 6, 10, 16, <u>26</u>, <u>42</u>, <u>68</u>, 110, . . .
   b. 3, 1, 4, 5, 9, 14, <u>23</u>, <u>37</u>, <u>60</u>, 97, . . .
   c. 3, 7, <u>10</u>, <u>17</u>, <u>27</u>, <u>44</u>, 71, . . .
   d. 1, 5, <u>6</u>, <u>11</u>, <u>17</u>, <u>28</u>, <u>45</u>, 73, . . .
   e. 6, <u>8</u>, 14, <u>22</u>, <u>36</u>, <u>58</u>, <u>94</u>, <u>152</u>, 246, . . .
   f. 2, <u>8</u>, 10, <u>18</u>, <u>28</u>, <u>46</u>, <u>74</u>, <u>120</u>, 194, . . .
   g. 6, <u>3</u>, <u>9</u>, 12, <u>21</u>, <u>33</u>, <u>54</u>, 87, . . .
   h. 1, <u>4</u>, <u>5</u>, <u>9</u>, 14, <u>23</u>, <u>37</u>, 60, . . .
   i. 3, <u>8</u>, <u>11</u>, <u>19</u>, 30, <u>49</u>, <u>79</u>, 128, . . .
   j. 6, <u>5</u>, <u>11</u>, <u>16</u>, <u>27</u>, <u>43</u>, <u>70</u>, <u>113</u>, 183, . . .
   k. 5, <u>3.5</u>, <u>8.5</u>, 12, <u>20.5</u>, <u>32.5</u>, 53, . . .
   l. Answers will vary.

More Than Graphs, Revised Edition • ©2004 Key Curriculum Press

Picturing Data: Scatter Plots and Line Graphs

STAT

Using Graphs to Picture Two-Variable Data

Setting the Stage

When you look at a set of numbers, what do you see? Probably not much, especially if there are very many numbers. A list of numbers can be confusing, and often not very interesting. Usually it's difficult to get a "picture" of what's happening. There are a variety of statistical graphs built into a graphing calculator that can help you picture data. In this activity and the next, you will learn how to use these statistical graphs.

The Activity

A Portland, Oregon, weather report in February listed the following temperatures in degrees Fahrenheit over a seven-day period.

How can you display this data to get a better picture of what's happening?

Date	High Temperature	Low Temperature
February 6	36	30
February 7	45	35
February 8	47	38
February 9	42	34
February 10	33	28
February 11	40	30
February 12	48	37

First you will need to store the data in your calculator. If your lists contain data, clear the lists. Then enter the dates in L1, the high temperatures in L2, and the low temperatures in L3. You will have to use a numeric format when entering the dates. One way to do this is to use 2.06 for February 6, 2.07 for February 7, etc. (You could also use 6, 7, 8, . . . for February 6, February 7, February 8, or 1, 2, 3, . . . for day 1, day 2, day 3, ...) Whatever you do, it will affect your WINDOW settings. After you've entered your data, your lists will look something like this:

The TI-73 and TI-83 can actually have titles as column headings. This is done by inserting a column on the TI-83 and then giving it a title, or just moving to the leftmost column of the TI-73 and giving that a title. Column titles should not exceed five letters in length.

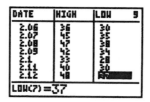

Press ⌐2nd⌐ [PLOT] or ⌐2nd⌐ [STAT PLOT]. Select a plotter by pressing 1, 2, or 3. Your calculator can plot up to three different statistics graphs at one time, although they will all be superimposed on each other. Once you have selected a plotter, several types of graphs are listed, depending on the type of calculator. When you turn on a plotter, you have a choice of

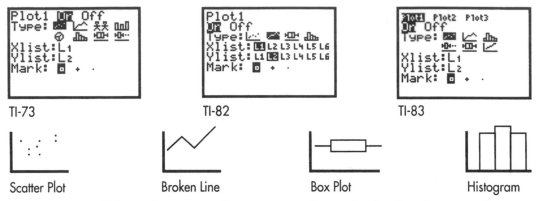

| TI-73 | TI-82 | TI-83 |

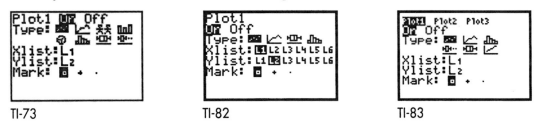

| Scatter Plot | Broken Line | Box Plot | Histogram |

In this activity you will learn how to make a scatter plot and a broken-line graph.

Scatter Plot

One way of picturing two-variable data is by using a scatter plot. Before plotting any data, however, be sure that all functions in Y= are cleared or turned off. You can do this by placing the cursor anywhere in the functions and pressing ⌐CLEAR⌐, or you can place the cursor over the equal sign, and press ⌐ENTER⌐ to deselect (turn off) the function. Press ⌐2nd⌐ [PLOT] or ⌐2nd⌐ [STAT PLOT] to access the STAT PLOTS menu. If any of the plots are on, turn them off by pressing ④ PlotsOff and then ⌐ENTER⌐. Access the STAT PLOTS menu again and press ①. You are now ready to set up Plot 1. To make a scatter plot that displays the date and the high temperatures, your screen should look something like this:

| TI-73 | TI-82 | TI-83 |

The TI-83 can access lists with data titles by inserting an L (LIST OPS B) and then typing in the title of the column.

The TI-73 uses the same process; press ⬚ 2nd [STAT] and select from the available choices.

Note that you can access only named lists that you have previously created.

Before plotting the data, you will need to input appropriate WINDOW settings. Do this. Then press ⬚GRAPH. Your window and graph might look like this:

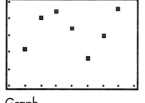

TI-73   TI-82/TI-83   Graph

On the TI-73, ΔX is a calculated value and is not entered by you.

Now make a scatter plot of the low temperatures. Do this by selecting Plot 2. Be sure to turn off Plot 1. What do you need to change in the Plot setup? Do you need to change your window?

If you choose different marks for Plot 1 and Plot 2 and turn on both plotters, you can display all of the points at once. Try this.

TI-73   TI-73

Or try it without column titles.

TI-83   TI-83

This might look very confusing to you. By changing the scatter plot to a broken-line graph, you will have a less-confusing picture of the data.

Broken-line Graphs

To make a line graph of the data, you only need to select a different graph icon in the Plot 1 and Plot 2 menus. Try this now.

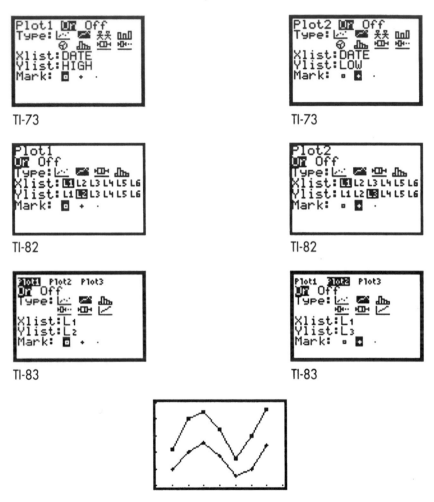

Practice Problem

Choose two different cities. Collect the high- and low-temperature data from your newspaper for seven days. Make a variety of scatter plots and line graphs to display the data. Write a paragraph describing at least four different things you noticed when looking at these graphs.

Extension Problem

Scatter plots and line graphs are often helpful for showing changes that occur over time.

An Experiment in Circulation

During a period of vigorous physical activity, your heart will beat faster in an effort to get oxygen to your muscle tissue. Record your resting pulse rate. Jump up and down on one foot for 30 sec and record the number of times your heart beats in a 5-sec time period by taking your own pulse.

Resting pulse rate: number of heartbeats in 5 sec _____

Time Intervals	Time Elapsed Since Exercise (in Seconds)	Number of Heart-beats in 5 Seconds
0	0	
1	15	
2	30	
3	45	
4	60	
5	75	
6	90	

Plot your data as a line graph. Sketch a picture of the graph indicating the WINDOW settings you used.

a. Does your heart return to its resting rate gradually or abruptly?

b. What effect do you think training or conditioning would have on the appearance of this graph?

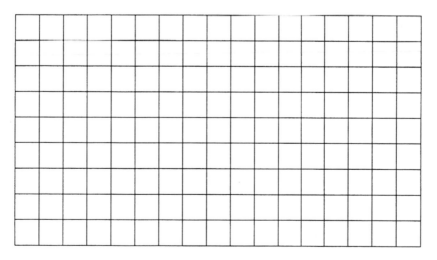

Picturing Data: Scatter Plots and Line Graphs

Objective:	To familiarize students with scatter plots and broken-line graphs
Materials needed:	TI-73, TI-82, TI-83, or TI-83 Plus graphing calculator
Appropriate level:	Algebra and pre-algebra
Time involved:	One hour or class period
Preparation:	Have weather data or some other statistics available

This is a lesson that should be taught early in the year for a number of reasons. It's not very difficult and doesn't require math skills that haven't been introduced as yet. Students will be introduced to some of the statisical features of the calculator, and quickly learn that it can do much more than simple calculations and graphing functions. A more compelling reason is that it's an activity that can be revisited during the year whenever new data is brought into the classroom, whether it's experimental data, test scores, athletic results, or budgeting concerns. It can be extended to enhance activities in other classes as well.

This may be the first time students have had experience with scatter plots. The scatter plots can be useful later as background when finding a line of best fit.

On the TI-73, TI-82, TI-83, and TI-83 Plus, Plots 1, 2, and 3 can be activated independently. It's possible to plot up to three sets of data at one time on the screen. If the data is non-

overlapping or uses different symbols, the lines should be easy to follow. Otherwise, great confusion can result.

When students enter data, they can view only three columns and seven entries at a time in the screen window. Seven days' data will fit exactly on the screen. You can actually enter up to 99 items in each list on the TI-82, and you can enter as many items as memory will allow on the TI-73 and TI-83. There are six numbered lists available. If students are going to examine more data, help them become comfortable with scrolling down the lists and across the columns using the arrow keys.

If you introduce large data sets, you might also want to have your students link their calculators to share data. The TI-GRAPH LINK™ is also very helpful when plotting data. It allows data or graphs to be printed or saved to a disk. It is compatible with both Macintosh and Windows environments.

More Than Graphs, Revised Edition • ©2004 Key Curriculum Press

Solutions

Practice Problem

Answers will vary.

Extension Problem

Answers will vary.

Picturing Data: Histograms and Box Plots

Using Graphs to Picture One-Variable Data

Setting the Stage

You can get a "picture" of one-variable data by constructing a histogram or a box plot. With a histogram, you can see how often a group of values occurs, while a box plot will show you how tightly the data is grouped about a middle value—the median—as well as how spread out the data is.

The data in the list below indicates the percentage of games won by each basketball team in the NBA before the playoffs.

Pacific Division		Midwest Division	
Phoenix	.754	Utah	.738
Seattle	.672	San Antonio	.707
L.A. Lakers	.610	Houston	.593
Portland	.542	Denver	.467
Sacramento	.492	Dallas	.386
Golden State	.305	Minnesota	.279
L.A. Clippers	.210		

Atlantic Division		Central Division	
Orlando	.770	Charlotte	.663
New York	.661	Indiana	.617
New Jersey	.410	Cleveland	.567
Boston	.400	Chicago	.508
Miami	.390	Atlanta	.500
Philadelphia	.283	Detroit	.383
Washington	.254	Milwaukee	.377

If you understand how these numbers are distributed, you may be better able to make a prediction about how the season will end.

The Activity

Histograms

You will need to clear any old data in L1 and enter these percentages. It makes no difference in what order you enter the data because you will be able to sort the numbers once they are entered. To do a *descending* sort, press ⟨STAT⟩ EDIT (⟨LIST⟩ on the TI-73). Choose SortD(L1) to put the percentages in order, with the highest number listed first. (This is ⟨STAT⟩ ⟨3⟩ ⟨2nd⟩ ⟨1⟩ on the TI-82 and TI-83, and ⟨2nd⟩ ⟨STAT⟩ OPS on the TI-73). If you choose SortA (L1), the calculator does an *ascending* sort and rebuilds the list with the lowest number listed first.

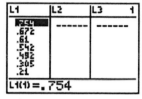

Before SortD (L1)   After SortD (L1)

Set the window as shown on one of the screens below.

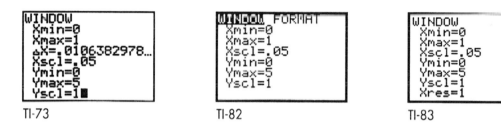

TI-73   TI-82   TI-83

Choose histogram as the graph type, L1 as the Xlist, and 1 for Freq. Press ⟨GRAPH⟩.

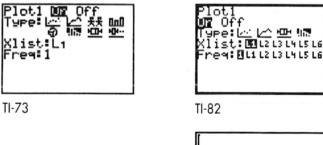

TI-73   TI-82   TI-83

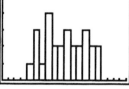

This kind of graph is called a **histogram**, and it is used to measure how many elements in a list fall within a certain interval. Because the *x*-values in this data represent percentages, these values must be between 0 and 1. Therefore, Xmin = 0 and Xmax = 1. So the right edge of the graph screen represents an *x*-value of 1.0 and the left edge is 0. The Xscl tells you that each bar is 0.05 unit wide. The Ymax setting must be larger than the number of values that are contained in the tallest bar. Sometimes you may have to guess an appropriate number for Ymax and adjust it after looking at the graph. If the top of the bar doesn't appear, increase Ymax. If the bars are too short, decrease Ymax. By looking at the marks at the left edge of this graph, you can see that in this case the largest number of teams in any group is four. If you press [TRACE] and then the right and/or left arrow keys, the *x*-values representing the right and left edges of the bar as well as the *y*-value, which tells you the number of elements in the bar, will be displayed.

Box Plots

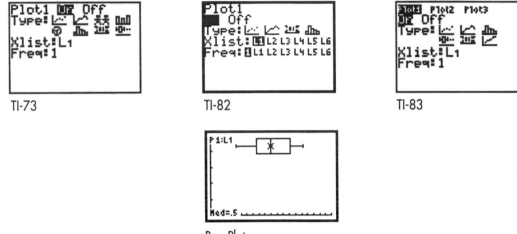

TI-73   TI-82   TI-83

Box Plot

Return to Plot 1, this time choosing the box plot icon. Press [GRAPH]. (Note: The values for Ymax and Ymin will not affect the box plot graph. However, to get the *x*-axis out of the way, it's best if you set Ymin to 0 and Ymax to something greater than 0. You will get an error if Ymin ≥ Ymax.) You will see a new display. The box plot, also called a box-and-whisker graph, divides the list, L1, into quartiles. The word *quartile* is used because the data is divided into four groups each containing 25% of the values.

Press [TRACE], and then the right and left arrows to see the values used to construct the box plot. The value on the end of the far-right whisker is the maximum value in the list. The value at the right-hand edge of the box marks the third quartile. The line in the middle of the box represents the median, which is the middle point in the data set.

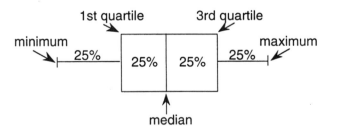

(If the data set contains an odd number of entries, then the median is the middle number. If there are an even number of entries, then average the two middle numbers to find the median.) One-half of the numbers are below the median value, and one-half are above. Also one-half of the data points are contained within the box. The left-hand edge of the box marks the first quartile. And the last value, which is at the end of the left whisker, is the minimum value. The length of the rectangle can give you an idea about how tightly the data is clustered around the middle value. And the distance between the whiskers shows you how spread out the data is.

Practice Problems

1. Experiment making different histograms using the data given above by changing the value of Xscl. (You may also have to change the value of Ymax.) Describe how these changes affect the appearance of the graph.
2. Collect some single-variable data from the sports page. Plot the data both as a histogram and box plot. Sketch the results in the windows that follow. Include the WINDOW settings for each graph. Explain what the Xscl value represents for the histogram. Describe how you determined the value for Ymax. For the box plot, name the five summary values: minimum, lower quartile, median, upper quartile, and maximum. Make some conjectures or conclusions based on each graph picture.

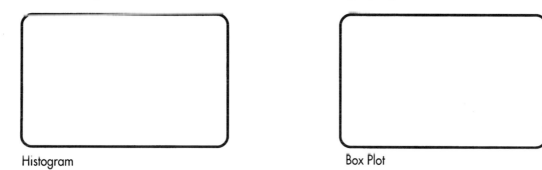

Histogram   Box Plot

Extension Problem

In many sports such as golf, swimming, track and field, distance running, basketball, and bowling, men and women compete under the same rules. By entering the men's data in one list and the women's data in the other list, it is possible to display a box plot for each list on the same screen by activating Plot 1 and Plot 2 at the same time.

Collect two sets of data—one for men and one for women—for the same sport. Plot the lists on the same screen using two different plots. Describe any similarities and/or differences that you notice.

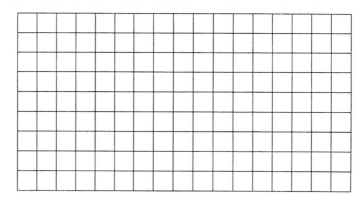

Picturing Data: Histograms and Box Plots

Objective:	To familiarize students with displays of one-dimensional variables
Materials needed:	TI-73, TI-82, TI-83, or TI-83 Plus graphing calculator
Appropriate level:	Algebra and pre-algebra
Time involved:	One hour or class period
Preparation:	Multiple copies of local sports pages need to be available

Learning how to graph data on the graphing calculator is not an easy task. A lot of thinking has to go into determining which kind of graph is best to show the information you have. Setting up the window is also a difficult task, particularly for the histogram. A shortcut is to use ZoomStat, but this teaches students nothing about intervals or neighborhoods. Encourage students to think about what the *x*-values represent. Remember that in a histogram, Xscl determines the width of the bar, and Ymax needs to be larger than the number of entries in the tallest column.

Students need to set the window so that all of the data points will fit. On the TI-82, TI-83, and TI-83 Plus, ZOOM 9:ZoomStat will do this; ZOOM 7:ZoomStat will do it on the TI-73. Don't introduce ZoomStat too early, however. Students will learn more from this activity if they have time to experiment and discover appropriate WINDOW settings.

Point out to students that they may be able to use the skills learned in this activity in other courses as well. They are likely to encounter data sets in social science courses as well as science courses.

Solutions

Practice Problems

Answers will vary.

Extension Problem

Answers will vary.

The Drawing Tablet

DRAW

Learning How to Draw Geometric Shapes

Setting the Stage

Did you know that artists often use mathematics when creating their works of art? In this activity, you will use math to draw pictures on your calculator. You will be able to store these pictures and write programs that can draw them on command. You will also be able to share your art with friends by downloading. If you have a computer and the appropriate software, you will even be able to print out a hard copy. Let your imagination run wild as you explore one of the many creative aspects of mathematics!

The Activity

Getting Set Up to Draw

The DRAW feature executes its commands on top of any graphics made by plotters in the STAT mode or graphs made with the Y= functions. For this reason, you must clear the Y= functions and turn all STAT PLOTS off (Choice 4) to have a blank screen for the drawing tablet.

You can eliminate the axes from the screen by going to [2nd] [FORMAT] and choosing AxesOff. (On the TI-82, press [WINDOW] [FORMAT] and then select AxesOff.)

You will also want to make sure that your WINDOW settings are friendly. For Quadrant I, these are the settings that will provide whole-number values for each pixel. The TI-73 actually has a setting (ZOOM 4) that will work for the first Quadrant, but it gives pixels in decimal values. On the TI-82 and TI-83, you can use the Splitscreen in the MODE menu so that you can see the graphics and Home screen areas at the same time.

```
WINDOW
 Xmin=0
 Xmax=94
 Xscl=0
 Ymin=0
 Ymax=62
 Yscl=0
 Xres=1
```

TI-82   TI-83

Experimenting with the DRAW Menu

Access the DRAW menu by pressing [2nd] [DRAW] (or just [DRAW] on the TI-73). What you see is a menu with a variety of features (8 on the TI-73; 11 on the TI-82 and TI-83). Commands will paint the screen in two colors, white (0) and black (1). Black is a default value, which means that it will be used unless white is specified. The white will essentially erase points.

You can enter drawing instructions directly from the keypad, or you can write a program. If you write a program to create a single object, later on you can write another program that calls on the previously written program so that you can build many objects at once. The larger program is often referred to as a *Macro*.

Before drawing objects or writing programs, you will need to become familiar with the DRAW features on your calculator. Have your calculator in hand to practice as you read. Unless otherwise noted, the command will work with the TI graphing calculators covered in this book.

1. ClrDraw: This one is easy. It just erases everything on the screen that was created with a Draw command. Plots and functions will clear and then be redrawn.

2. Line: The Line command, Line (X1, Y1, X2, Y2), will draw a black line from point (X1, Y1) to point (X2, Y2). These numbers can be entered directly or brought in as program variables.
   Example: Line (0, 0, 40, 30) will draw a black line from (0, 0) to (40, 30). It will have a length of 50.

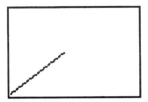 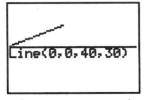

Fullscreen on TI-73, TI-82, and TI-83   Splitscreen on TI-82 and TI-83

Note: When you press (ENTER) to execute a Line command, you will be on the graph screen. To return to the Home screen, press (2nd) [QUIT].

Line (8, 6, 24, 18, 0) will create what appears to be a gap within this line segment. This is the closest the Drawing tablet can come to erasing.

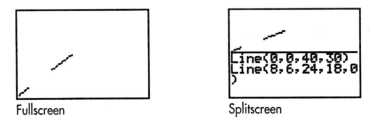

Fullscreen   Splitscreen

3. Horizontal: Horizontal creates a left-to-right line that will move up and down the screen with the cursor. When the appropriate cursor position is reached, press (ENTER). Each ENTER will create a new line.

4. Vertical: Vertical creates an up-and-down line that will move left and right with the cursor. It is also dropped with an ENTER command.

5. Tangent (not on TI-73): Tangent lines will touch any curve you have graphed at exactly one point, which you must choose. Enter a function such as $y = 50 \sin (.1x)$ in Y=. Press (GRAPH) and use the TRACE function to put the cursor on the point where you want to draw the tangent line. Select Tangent from the DRAW menu to draw the tangent line.

6. DrawF (not on TI-73): This command will draw functions. DrawF x^2 will draw the function $y = x^2$. You can also use DrawF to draw functions that you have entered into Y= earlier. If you have entered several functions in Y=, you can specify which one you want drawn by choosing DrawF and then using [Y-VARS] to select the function you want to draw.

7. Shade: The Shade command is Shade (Y1,Y2, res, L, R). For the TI-73, the command is Shade (Y1, Y2, L, R, Pattern, res) where Pattern is (1) vertical; (2) horizontal; (3) diagonal, upper-left to lower-right; (4) diagonal, lower-left to upper-right. This will shade the area above Y1 and below Y2. These functions may also be entered directly into the Shade command. The resolution number (0–9) will allow different levels of shading. If you do not enter a resolution, it reverts to the default value of 1. L stands for the left limit, and R stands for the right limit.

8. DrawInv (not on TI-73): This option allows you to draw the inverse of a function. Enter $y1 = x^2$. DrawInv Y1 will graph the inverse of Y1, which is $y = \sqrt{x}$. If Y2 = 2x, DrawInv Y2 will graph $y = \frac{x}{2}$.

9. Circle: There are two approaches to drawing a circle. If you are on the graph screen and you select Circle from the DRAW menu, a cursor will appear on the screen. Position the cursor at the center of the circle you want to draw and press ⬚ENTER⬚. Move the cursor to a point you want to be on the circle and press ⬚ENTER⬚ again. The calculator will then draw the circle.

   If you are on the Home screen and select Circle from the DRAW menu, you can specify the center and radius. Circle (x, y, z) will draw a circle with its center at the point (x, y) and radius z. For example, Circle (10, 15, 8) will create a circle of radius 8 around the point (10, 15).

10. Text: Text can be entered two ways. To enter text directly onto a graph, place the cursor where you want the text to begin, and select Text from the DRAW menu. Press ⬚ENTER⬚ when you are done entering your text. You can also enter text within a program or from the Home screen with the command Text (x, y, "Text"). For example, (0, 0, "origin") will place a label at the origin. This is a very nice feature when printing hard copy!

11. Pen: Pen will allow a free pen to draw across the screen. Select Pen and press ⬚ENTER⬚ to turn the drawing tool on and off. Use the cursors to move across the screen.

Storing and Recalling Pictures

There is no undo command on the keyboard, and erasing is not an easy process. One way of protecting work is to store the pictures so that you can retrieve or recreate certain steps without having to start over from scratch.

Storing Pictures

Under the DRAW menu, press the right arrow to choose the STORE menu (STO).

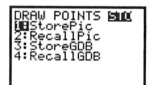

Select (StorePic).

(The Graphics DataBase [GDB] setting on the TI-82, TI-83, and TI-83 Plus will actually store WINDOW and plotter settings for easy retrieval later when studying new data.)

On the TI-83 and TI-73, choose a number in which to store your picture (0–9 on the TI-83; 1–3 on the TI-73). For example, if you enter 3 the calculator will store the picture to Pic3. Choose one of these picture slots in which to store the screen, but make sure you aren't storing on top of a previously stored screen.

On the TI-82, you cannot just type the number of the picture slot as above; you must use the picture variable, such as Pic3. To access picture variables, press (VARS) and select (4) (Picture).

Choose one of the picture slots.

Press (ENTER) once to return to the Home screen and once more to execute the storage.

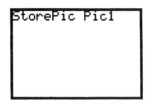

Recalling Pictures

Choose STO under the DRAW menu and select ②（RecallPic). Type the number of the picture slot that you want to recall (on the TI-82, press [VARS] [4] to select the picture variable).

Practice Problems

1. Draw each of these figures on your calculator. On separate paper, list the instructions you used. (Graph paper or geoboards may be helpful.)
   a. a rectangle with vertices at (3, 5), (3, 25), (33, 25), and (33, 5)
   b. a triangle with vertices at (0, 0), (24, 16), and (16, 24)
   c. a figure 8 (two circles, one above the other) along the line $x = 10$
   d. a circle inscribed in a square, both centered around the point (10, 10)
   e. a circle circumscribed about a triangle with vertices at (10, 10), (10, 50), and (30, 30)
   f. the Olympic symbol (five interlocking rings)
2. How do you know that the line from (0, 0) to (40, 30) is really 50 units in length?
3. Describe what actually happens when a line is "erased."

Extension Problems

If you create separate programs to draw a triangle, square, and circle, you can create a new program that can call up each of these shapes. For example, you can create a program called Shapes, made up of programs such as Tri, Sqr, and Circ.

Example: PROGRAM: SHAPES
             :prgmTRI
             :prgmSQR
             :prgmCIRC

Experienced programmers can even program their shapes using variables for vertices, so the shapes can be "moved" by redefining the variables within the program.

1. Describe three different strategies for making a square appear on the screen. Record the necessary steps.
2. Which of the strategies you named in Problem 1 should you use if you wish the square to be shaded? Record the steps necessary to shade the square.
3. Write a separate program to construct each shape shown.

4. Write another program that incorporates your programs from Problem 3, and draw a design on the calculator screen.
5. Write a program to create a picture of your own using what you've learned in this activity.

The Drawing Tablet

Objective: To learn about the DRAW commands and construct geometric shapes
Materials needed: TI-73, TI-82, TI-83, or TI-83 Plus graphing calculator, possibly graph paper
Appropriate level: Algebra and pre-algebra
Time involved: Two hours minimum
Preparation: Familiarity with a variety of geometric terms and concepts (*point, line, radius, tangent, vertex . . .*)

Students really enjoy this activity—even those students who are not usually turned on by math. They become very involved, sometimes putting much more effort into it than what was intended. You may wish to encourage your students to do independent projects over an extended period of time. At my school, we had a TI-picture contest with prizes for the top three winners. The more impressive pictures from our contest came from students who drew their pictures first on graph paper using a 94 by 62 coordinate system. A first-quadrant numbering system seemed to work best (0–94 by 0–62). Negative numbers really slowed down their creativity.

My students figured out that they could build maze-type games with this imagery. By calling up images from within a program they could create different obstacles in each room. Students shared many of their ideas and creations with each other both in hard copy and by linking images. We got into some very good discussions about the effect of light sources and shading, projection and perspectives, and shortcuts to the programming process when using The Drawing Tablet.

Because of this lesson we decided that we simply must have software to print hard copies of the pictures and to store data to a disk. The pictures the students were making were using up too much memory just to keep them stored on the calculator. The TI-GRAPH LINK™ allows you to store these pictures and programs on a computer.

The Drawing Tablet shouldn't be rushed. Take time to talk about each command. Allow a lot of time for practice and encourage discussions among students and groups. This unit truly teaches patience.

Solutions

(Answers for these problems will vary.)

Practice Problems

1. a. Line (3, 5, 3, 25)
   Line (3, 25, 33, 25)
   Line (33, 25, 33, 5)
   Line (33, 5, 3, 5)

   b. Line (0, 0, 24, 16)
   Line (16, 24, 24, 16)
   Line (16, 24, 0, 0)

   c. Sample
   Circle (10, 5, 5)
   Circle (10, 15, 5)

   d. Sample
   Circle (10, 10, 5)
   Line (5, 5, 5, 15)
   Line (5, 15, 15, 15)
   Line (15, 15, 15, 5)
   Line (15, 5, 5, 5)

   e. Circle (30, 10, 20)
   Line (10, 10, 10, 50)
   Line (10, 50, 30, 30)
   Line (30, 30, 10, 10)

   f. Sample
   Circle (10, 30, 10)
   Circle (26, 30, 10)
   Circle (42, 30, 10)
   Circle (18, 14, 10)
   Circle (34, 14, 10)

2. Create a triangle with vertices (0, 0), (30, 40), and (40, 0). This is a right triangle and the unknown distance is the missing side.
   $(30 - 0)^2 + (40 - 0)^2 = 50^2$ (the Pythagorean theorem)

3. A line is not erased; the pixels in the specified location are turned off.

Extension Problems

Answers will vary.

The Tortoise and the Hare

Finding Common Solutions with a Third Variable

Setting the Stage

Harry the Hare challenges Tina the Tortoise to a race on a 20-m track. The day of the race, Tina jumps off to a quick lead, burning up the track at a blistering 0.2 m/sec. Harry the Hare, supreme in his overconfidence, remains at the starting line boasting to the crowd in the bleachers, delaying his start for an additional 90 sec. If Harry's top speed is 1 m/sec, can he still win the race?

The Activity

You can view this race using parametric equations on your calculator. These are equations that use a third variable, t, to study x and y. In this situation, t represents the time, x represents the distance run, and y represents the track number of the contestant. Press [MODE] and change the settings to **Parametric** and **Simultaneous**.

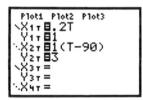

Use the WINDOW settings [0, 150, 1, 0, 30, 10, ⁻2, 4, 1]. Enter these equations after pressing [Y=].

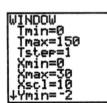

Upper Window

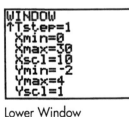

Lower Window

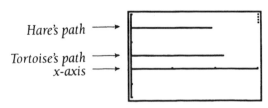

$X_{1T} = 0.2t$	Tina the Tortoise moves at a slow and steady pace.
$Y_{1T} = 1$	This places the tortoise in lane 1.
$X_{2T} = 1(t - 90)$	Harry the Hare waits 90 sec before running.
$Y_{2T} = 3$	This places the hare in lane 3.

Push [GRAPH] to watch the race unfold. Try to determine if the hare overtakes the tortoise before or after the 20-m distance. Remember that the hare does not begin to run until 90 sec after the

starter's gun is fired. If you want to watch an "instant replay" of the race, turn X_{1T} off and then turn it back on. Use [TRACE] for a "slow motion" replay. Use the up and down arrows to switch from track to track.

The hash marks on the x-axis are in 10-m units.

Hare's path ⟶

Tortoise's path ⟶
x-axis ⟶

More Than Graphs, Revised Edition • ©2004 Key Curriculum Press

Press [2nd] [TABLE] to see a printout of the time values, t, plotted against x. Use the right arrow key to see the values for X2T and Y2T. Notice that at 112.5 sec, the tortoise and the hare have traveled the same distance, 22.5 m. Because the race is only 20 m in length, Tina the Tortoise will win.

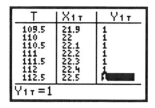
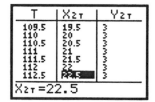

Practice Problems

1. How far had Tina run when Harry started his sprint?
2. If Harry the Hare were less boastful, he might have been able to win the race. How long could Harry actually have waited and still won? Test your theory by running the race again with different equations for Harry.
3. Tammy the Tortoise is even faster than her sister, Tina, so she challenges Harry to a race over an even-greater distance, 30 m. Tammy can run at 0.3 m/sec. Harry, remembering that he passed Tina after 22.5 m, is again boastful and overconfident. He once more delays for 90 sec before starting his sprint. Press (WINDOW) and set Tmax = 200 and Xmax = 35 to extend the track.
   a. Who wins this race?
   b. How long does the race last?
   c. At the end of the race, how far behind is the slower contestant?

Extension Problems

A freight train, a passenger train, and a passenger van all travel southbound from Seattle to California. The freight train leaves Seattle at 6 a.m. and proceeds at an average speed of 40 mi/hr. The passenger train leaves Seattle at 8 a.m. and travels at an average speed of 60 mi/hr. The van leaves Seattle at 9 a.m. and travels at an average speed of 70 mi/hr.

1. Record your window and the equations you use here.
2. Portland, Oregon, is 200 mi south of Seattle. Which vehicle arrives in Portland first?
3. How many miles south of Seattle does the passenger train overtake the freight train?
4. At what time does that occur?
5. How many miles south of Seattle does the van pass the passenger train?

The Tortoise and the Hare

Objective: To create a visual model of parametric equations
Materials needed: TI-82, TI-83, or TI-83 Plus graphing calculator
Appropriate level: Algebra and pre-algebra
Time involved: One class period
Preparation: Familiarity with distance, speed, time relationship

Although it's not common to study parametrics at an algebra or pre-algebra level, this activity provides an introduction to the topic as well as reinforcing students' understanding of the distance, speed, and time relationship. Students learn how to define equations in terms of time (t) and watch a simulation of the experiment on the screen. They enjoy actually being able to watch the race unfold.

Care should be taken to ensure that the MODE is set as Simultaneous, and not Sequential. This allows all the formulas to be calculated concurrently as the events would actually happen.

Solutions

Practice Problems

1. 10 m
2. Harry can wait 80 sec and tie, so he should wait slightly less than 80 sec.
3. a. Tammy wins.
   b. The race lasts 100 sec.
   c. Harry will have run only 10 m.

Extension Problems

1. [0, 10, 1, 0, 500, 10, 0, 6, 1]
   $X1T = 40t$ $X2T = 60(t - 2)$ $X3T = 70(t - 3)$
   $Y1T = 1$ $Y2T = 3$ $Y3T = 5$
2. The freight train arrives in Portland first.
3. 280 mi south
4. 3 mi/hr
5. 420 mi

Hidden Digits

Discovering the True Accuracy of Displayed Decimal Numbers

Setting the Stage

Most calculators display numbers up to about eight decimal places. If a number is too large or too small for the display to show the significant digits, the calculator will use scientific notation. Eight decimal places is usually more than enough accuracy, but you may be curious about how many digits are "hiding" in the calculator.

You can test your calculator to see how many digits it will display by pressing [2nd] [π]. Count the number of digits that appear on the screen. How many are on the display? The number π is an irrational number, which means that it has no exact decimal value. So any value for π that appears on the calculator will only be an approximation of its exact value. This is also true of some rational numbers because the calculator often is not able to display all of a number's digits. However, your calculator is remembering more than it is showing. There are other digits of π not visible on the screen that the calculator knows but isn't letting you see. Is there some way you can make the calculator show the missing digits?

The Activity

Press [2nd] [π] [ENTER] to see the value of π.

Record the value: π is approximately (≈) _____

This is not the exact value of π. It's not even the calculator's best estimate. In this activity you will explore some strategies that will allow you to see the hidden digits.

Press ([2nd] [ANS] − 3) · 10. Press [ENTER] and record the result. _____

   (Note: If you press [2nd] [ANS], the calculator will display the last value it calculated, and you can do further calculations on it.)

How is this string of digits different from the value of π that the calculator displayed? When the calculator displayed the original value of π, the last digit was 4. Now the last two digits are 36.

Press [2nd] [ENTRY] and edit the expression on the screen so that it reads ([2nd] [ANS] − 1) · 10. Press [ENTER] and record the result. _____

How does this answer compare to the previous result?

How can you determine which number to subtract each time?

Press 2nd [ENTRY] again and edit the expression to read (2nd [ANS] – 4) · 10. Press ENTER and record the result. _____

Did any new digits appear? If they did, then continue this process until no new digits appear.

What is the value of π stored by your calculator?

Practice Problems

1. Another irrational number stored in your calculator is $\sqrt{5}$. You can display this number by pressing 2nd [$\sqrt{}$] 5. Use a procedure similar to the one in the activity to find the hidden digits.
2. Find the hidden digits for each number. Note: To calculate the cube root of a number, press MATH 4.

	Displayed Value	Stored Value
$\sqrt{2}$		
$\sqrt[3]{11}$		
$\frac{9}{7}$		
$\sqrt{3}$		
$\sqrt[3]{4}$		

Extension Problems

In Problems 1 through 4 you will explore how you can use the *iPart* command to reveal any hidden digits.

1. Press MATH NUM 3 2nd [π] ENTER (MATH NUM 2 2nd [π] ENTER on the TI-82). What is the result? _____
2. Find the *iPart* of 123.456789. What is the result?_____
3. Explain what the *iPart* command does. Experiment a few more times to be sure.
4. Enter $\pi \cdot 10^9 - iPart(\pi \cdot 10^9)$ to see the digits that the calculator was hiding. What is the result? If the first of these digits is greater than 4, the calculator will round up the last digit in the simplified display.
5. Create your own method for finding hidden digits. Clearly explain how and why your method works.

TEACHER NOTES

Hidden Digits

Objective:	To discover the true accuracy of displayed decimal numbers
Materials needed:	TI-73, TI-82, TI-83, or TI-83 Plus graphing calculator
Appropriate level:	Algebra and pre-algebra
Time involved:	One hour or one class period
Preparation:	Some introduction to irrational numbers

Hidden Digits examines some of the problems of using estimated values to replace irrational numbers. Most early calculators printed values of six to eight places. How close is the calculator value to the real one? How close is the value we see to the value it retains in memory? In the case of a repeating decimal, missing digits can usually be reconstructed from what is already visible. With an irrational number, such as π, you cannot predict what the unseen digits will be.

Students will probably be surprised when they find out that the calculator actually computes using more digits than it displays. They should also gain some insights into how the calculator rounds the last digit in a displayed number.

The value of π stored by the calculator is 3.1415926535898.

Solutions

Practice Problems

1. 2.360679774998
2.

	Displayed Value	Stored Value
$\sqrt{2}$	1.414213562	1.4142135623731
$\sqrt[3]{11}$	2.223980091	2.2239800905693
$\frac{9}{7}$	1.285714286	1.2857142857143
$\sqrt{3}$	1.732050808	1.7320508075689
$\sqrt[3]{4}$	1.587401052	1.5874010519682

Extension Problems

1. 3
2. 123
3. The calculator displays only the integer part of the number.
4. 0.5898

Primes and Composites

Using a Program to Prime Factor a Number

Setting the Stage

Identifying prime numbers, particularly the largest-known prime number, has long been a recreational activity for mathematicians. The advent of computer technology has made it possible for mathematicians and others to successfully search for larger and larger primes. You may think that this is not a very worthwhile activity, but prime numbers are used today when developing elaborate secret code systems.

I think I'll cancel tennis today and look for some primes.

The Activity

A **prime** number has only two divisors—the number 1 and itself. Any whole number that is not prime is called a **composite**. The number 1 is neither prime nor composite. A composite number is any number that can be written as a product of prime number factors. To find the prime factorization of a composite number you could make a number tree. To do this you divide a number by one of its factors, divide each resulting factor by one of their factors, and continue this process until all of the factors are prime numbers. See if you can follow the steps used to factor the number 48.

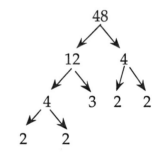

Thus, 48 can be written as $2 \times 2 \times 2 \times 2 \times 3$, or, using exponents, $48 = 2^4 \times 3$.

Use this method to find the prime factorization of 72. Even with a calculator, this can be a tedious process, especially with large numbers, and particularly if the prime factors of a number are large prime numbers. Try using your calculator and making a factor tree to find the prime factorization of 14,162.

You probably tried dividing by 2 first, the result being $14,162 = 2 \times 7081$. After trying a number of factors, did you give up before finding that 73 is a factor of 7081? The prime factorization of 14,162 is $2 \times 73 \times 97$.

A calculator program can speed up this process. Enter the program PRIME and use it to find the prime factorization of each number given in the practice problems.

TI-82/TI-83 Program

Program: PRIMES
ClrHome
Disp "PRIME FACTORS OF"
Input A
A→N
{1}→L1
1→F
2→D
While D<√(A)
While fPart(N/D)=0
D→L1(F)
F+1→F
N/D→N
End
D+1→D
End
If N>1
N→L1(F)
Disp L1

TI-73 Program

Program: PRIMES
ClrScreen
Disp "PRIME FACTORS"
Disp "OF"
Input A
A→N
{1}→L1
1→F
2→D
While (D<√(A))
While fPart(N/D)=0
D→L1(F)
(F+1)→F
(N/D)→N
End
D+1→D
End
If N>1
N→L1(F)
Disp L1
Pause

This program will calculate the prime factors, store the factors in L1, and display them in a horizontal list on the screen. If the list of factors is "too wide" for the screen, press `2nd` [L1] `ENTER` (`2nd` [STAT] and select L1 on the TI-73), and use the right and left arrows to scroll through the list. You can check that the product of the prime factors is the original number by pressing `2nd` [LIST] MATH `6` `2nd` [L1] `ENTER` (TI-82 and TI-83 only).

Practice Problems

Find the prime factorization of each number.

1. 60
2. 320
3. 108
4. 94
5. 144
6. 234
7. 678
8. 8540
9. 2735
10. 34,563

Extension Problems

1. Do some research and find out what the largest-known prime number is, who found it, and how much computer time it took.
2. Do some research and find out how prime numbers are used when developing secret codes.
3. Explain in your own words how the program works.
4. Explain how you could modify this program to help you reduce a fraction to simplest terms.

Primes and Composites

Objective: To use a program to assist in the prime factorization of large numbers
Materials needed: TI-73, TI-82, TI-83, or TI-83 Plus graphing calculator
Appropriate level: Algebra and pre-algebra
Time involved: One hour or class period
Preparation: Some familiarity with prime numbers and number trees

Most students are already familiar with factor trees as a means of finding prime factors. This program lets the student see how quickly the calculator can look for factors by electronic guess-and-check. The calculator starts by repeatedly dividing by 2 until a remainder occurs, then it divides by 3, then 4 . . . until the divisor equals the square root of the number being factored. At that point all integral factors will have been listed on the screen.

One interesting observation of this program is its brutality in testing every consecutive integer as a factor. It relies completely on the strength and speed of the machinery for grinding out solutions. If 2, 3, and 5 have already been tested as factors for a number and failed, there is really no need to test for 6, 8, 9, or 10 as factors. This program tests those values anyway before continuing, if only for the sake of simplicity in building the initial program. A more elegant program would take the earlier tests into consideration in order to speed up the factor search. For students who find this interesting, it may be useful to point out that designing efficient search patterns is a major concern when programming.

Solutions

Practice Problems

1. $2^2 \times 3 \times 5$
2. $2^6 \times 5$
3. $2^2 \times 3^3$
4. 2×47
5. $2^4 \times 3^2$
6. $2 \times 3^2 \times 13$
7. $2 \times 3 \times 113$
8. $2^2 \times 5 \times 7 \times 61$
9. 5×547
10. $3 \times 41 \times 281$

Extension Problems

Answers will vary.

The Euclidean Algorithm

PROG

Finding the GCD of Large Numbers

Setting the Stage

When you name all of the factors of two or more numbers, you will often find that there is a set of common factors. The largest common factor is called the *greatest common divisor,* or GCD, and it is very useful when you work with fractions with different denominators. In this activity, you will first find GCDs using your calculator to factor numbers. Then you will use a method for finding the Greatest Common Divisor that was first described by Euclid in his book *The Elements.*

Euclid was a Greek mathematician who lived in Alexandria around 300 B.C. He is most famous for having written *The Elements,* in which he stated the groundwork for what we now call *Euclidean geometry.* Euclid also devoted several books of *The Elements* to number theory, and in one of these he describes a way to determine the greatest common divisor of two numbers. This method is now called the *Euclidean algorithm,* and it is still considered the most effective way to find the greatest common divisor.

The Activity

If you want to find the GCD of 48 and 36, you could first find all of the factors of 48. They are 1, 2, 3, 4, 6, 8, 12, 16, 24, and 48. The factors of 36 are 1, 2, 3, 4, 6, 9, 12, 18, and 36. The common factors of the two numbers are 1, 2, 3, 4, 6, and 12. Therefore, the largest common factor of 48 and 36 is 12. This is shown in the Venn diagram at the right.

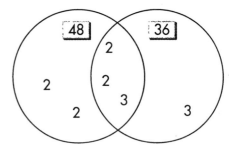

A more elegant approach is to find the prime factors of each number. Factoring, we get $48 = 2 \cdot 2 \cdot 2 \cdot 2 \cdot 3$ and $36 = 2 \cdot 2 \cdot 3 \cdot 3$. If you were to show this in a Venn diagram, you would see that 48 and 36 share two factors of 2 and one factor of 3. The Venn diagram looks like this:

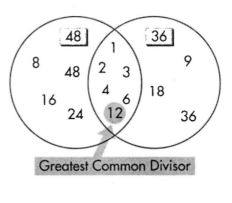

If you multiply the common prime factors together, you get the GCD, which is $2 \cdot 2 \cdot 3 = 12$.

More Than Graphs, Revised Edition • ©2004 Key Curriculum Press

Even with a calculator, finding all of the prime factors of two numbers and then finding the ones they have in common can be very tedious, especially if the numbers are very large. The Euclidean algorithm is a much more efficient method. To use this method, you start by dividing the smaller number into the larger number, making note of the remainder. You then divide the remainder into the previous dividend, again remembering the remainder. You repeat this process until the remainder is 0. The dividend when this happens is the GCD. If this sounds confusing, look at this example to see how it's done.

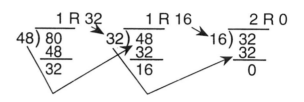

Find the GCD of 80 and 48 using the Euclidean algorithm.

When the divisor is equal to 16, the remainder is 0, so the GCD of 48 and 80 is 16.

It is easy to program a calculator to do the Euclidean algorithm because it involves doing the same thing over and over again. See if you can figure out how the GCD program works.

TI-82/TI-83 Program

```
PROGRAM:GCD
ClrHome
Lbl 1
Input "LARGER NUMBER? ",A
Input "SMALLER NUMBER? ",B
If B>A
Goto 1
A→S
B→R
While R>0
S→L
R→S
iPart(L/S)→Q
L-SQ→R
End
Disp "GCD=",S
Disp "LCM=",AB/S
```

TI-73 Program

```
PROGRAM:GCD
ClrScreen
Lbl 1
Input "LARGER NUMBER? ",A
Input "SMALLER NUMBER? ",B
If B>A
Goto 1
A→S
B→R
While R>0
S→L
R→S
iPart(L/S) Q
L-SQ→R
End
Disp "GCD=",S
Disp "LCM=",AB/S
Pause
```

Practice Problems

1. Use the program PRIMES, which you entered in the Primes and Composites activity, to find the GCD of each pair of numbers. Draw a Venn diagram to display your results.
   a. 64 and 30
   b. 21 and 315
   c. 103 and 78
   You may want to use the program PRIMES for Problems 2 and 3.

2. Sometimes one of the numbers is a factor of the other. If you wanted to find the GCD of 15 and 30, you would note that 15 is the largest factor of both numbers. Draw a Venn diagram showing the prime factors for a pair of numbers in which the smaller number is the GCD of the two numbers.

3. If the only common factor of the numbers is 1, they are said to be *relatively prime*. For example, 63 and 32 have no common factors other than 1, and though neither is prime, they are relatively prime. Draw a Venn diagram showing the prime factors for a pair of numbers that are relatively prime.

4. Use the GCD program to find the greatest common divisor of each pair of numbers.
   a. 630 and 875
   b. 864 and 936
   c. 4,212 and 5,200
   d. 1,701 and 1,260
   e. 8,464 and 11,500
   f. 3,795 and 3,432
   g. 6,355 and 5,822
   h. 4,652 and 3,417
   i. 6,327 and 5,700
   j. 10,088 and 9,048

Extension Problems

The **least common multiple** of two numbers is the smallest number that can be divided by each of the numbers without having any remainders. It is not necessarily the product of the two numbers. If you multiply 9 and 12, for example, the product is 108. But 36 is a much smaller number that can be divided evenly by both 9 and 12. Again look at a Venn diagram to see what is happening.

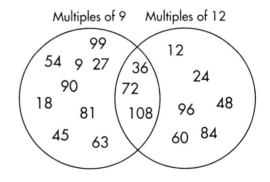

Because the list of multiples goes on and on, only some of the multiples have been shown in each circle. However, you can see that even though 9 · 12 = 108 is a common multiple, there are two other common multiples that are smaller.

On the TI-73, both LCM and GCD are library functions that reside within the calculator. To find the least common multiple of 14 and 21, press MATH 1, enter "14, 21" (the order of the numbers is unimportant), and press ENTER to see an answer.

An easy way for the calculator to find the least common multiple (LCM) of two numbers is to divide their product by their GCD.

1. Use the GCD program to find the least common multiple of each pair of numbers in Practice Problem 4.
2. Explain why it works to divide the product of a pair of numbers by the greatest common divisor to find the least common multiple.

TEACHER NOTES

The Euclidean Algorithm

Objective: To find greatest common divisors of large numbers
Materials needed: TI-73, TI-82, TI-83, or TI-83 Plus graphing calculator
Appropriate level: Algebra and pre-algebra
Time involved: One hour or class period
Preparation: An understanding of divisors and common denominators

The traditional method for finding the greatest common divisor (GCD) is to build a number tree of prime factors for each term, and then note how many of each they both have in common, and multiply those prime factors. This works, but can take a long time and is not particularly elegant or inspiring. The Euclidean algorithm is a much more economical approach, as long as the computations involved in division are not an obstacle. This makes it perfectly suited for a programmable calculator.

Likewise, one method of finding common multiples of two terms is to create a list of multiples.

If the GCD can be easily found, the LCM can be quickly calculated by taking the product of any two numbers and dividing by their GCD. This is what the end of the program does.

If the students understand the algorithms, then figuring out how the program works is fairly simple. This is a good program to ask students to analyze, as this will give them some insights into how programs are designed.

The PRIMES program can be found in the Primes and Composites activity.

Solutions

Practice Problems

1. a. 2
    b. 21
    c. 1
2. Answers will vary.
3. Answers will vary.
4. See table next page.

Extension Problems

1. See table next page.
2. Answers will vary. A Venn diagram may be very useful in explaining this. When you multiply the two numbers together, the result is the product of all their factors, including factors that are duplicated. When you divide this by the GCD, you divide out all of the factors that were duplicated, leaving each factor of each number represented only one time.

	Solutions to Practice Problems (GCDs)	Solutions to Extension Problems (LCMs)
a.	35	15,750
b.	2	11,262
c.	52	411,200
d.	63	34,020
e.	92	1,058,000
f.	33	394,680
g.	41	902,410
h.	1	15,895,884
i.	57	632,700
j.	104	877,656

Playing the Numbers

Predicting and Estimating Using Number Theory

Setting the Stage

Pythagoras founded a religious, scientific, and philosophical brotherhood that was really a formal school. These early Pythagoreans noticed many intriguing relationships in numbers, and they believed that numbers were the essence of the universe. Some historians say the teachings of the group were kept secret by the members. One such relationship involves perfect numbers. A number that equals the sum of its divisors including 1, but not the number itself, is called *perfect*. The number 6 is the smallest perfect number. Numbers that are larger than the sum of their divisors are called abundant, and numbers less than the sum are called deficient. Two numbers are called *amicable* or *friendly* if each is equal to the sum of the divisors of the other, for example, 284 and 220. In this activity, you will use your calculator to play a game with perfect numbers.

Game Rules

Number of players: two or four. If there are four players, divide into two teams with two people on each team.

The object of the game is to determine whether the sum of the factors of a number is greater than the number, less than the number, or equal to the number. (Note: For this game, the sum of the factors does not include the number itself.) Paper and pencil for calculations are not allowed. Play starts with the number 10. Players should flip a coin to determine who goes first. The first player starts with the numbers 10 and 11. A player tries to predict whether the sum of the factors for each of the numbers will be greater than, less than, or equal to the number itself. *For each correct answer, the player scores 2 points.* In addition, if the player can name the sum of the factors, he or she scores an extra 5 points per number. If the player correctly identifies a number as being a prime, he or she adds another 3 points to his or her score.

One player should run the program while the other player records each player's (or team's) score in a separate list on the calculator. To access the STAT List, press `STAT` `1` (`LIST` on the TI-73). Be sure the lists are cleared when you begin each game. To do this, move the cursor to the L at the top of the list, and press `CLEAR` `ENTER`. At the end of the game, use sum(L1) (or L2, etc.) to total each player's (or team's) score. This command is [2nd] [LIST] MATH [5] ([2nd] [STAT] MATH [7] on the TI-73). Players can alternate calculator tasks during the game. Be sure to use one calculator for running the program and another calculator for keeping score. Otherwise, you will erase your scores when you run the program. (If you have only one calculator, do not store any scores in L1.) Record the results for each number in the table.

After you enter a number and run the program, if there are so many factors that you can't see them all on the screen, press [2nd] [L1] ([2nd] [STAT] and select L1 on the TI-73) and use the right and left arrow keys to scroll through the list. Or you can press [STAT] [1] and view the list of factors in L1 on the TI-82 and TI-83. Press [LIST] on the TI-73.

TI-82/TI-83 Program

```
PROGRAM:PERFECT
ClrList L1
ClrHome
Input "NUMBER>1?",N
1→L1(1)
2→F
2→D
While D<N
While fPart(N/D)=0
D→L1(F)
(D+1)→D
(F+1)→F
End
(D+1)→D
End
If N>1
N→L1(F)
Disp "ALL FACTORS ARE:"
Disp L1
(sum(L1)-N)→S
Disp "FACTOR SUM =",S
If S=N
Disp "IT IS PERFECT"
If S>N
Disp "EXCESSIVE"
If S<N and S≠1
Disp "DEFECTIVE"
If S=1
Disp "PRIME"
```

TI-73 Program

```
PROGRAM:PERFECT
QuadReg L1
ClrScreen
Input "NUMBER>1?",N
1→L1(1)
2→F
2→D
While D<N
While fPart(N/D)=0
D→L1(F)
(D+1)→D
(F+1)→F
End
(D+1)→D
End
If N>1
N→L1(F)
Disp "ALL FACTORS ARE"
Disp L1
(sum(L1)-N)→S
Disp "FACTOR SUM=",S
If S=N
Disp "IT IS PERFECT"
If S>N
Disp "EXCESSIVE"
If S<N and S≠1
Disp "DEFECTIVE"
If S=1
Disp "PRIME"
Pause
```

Extension Problems

1. Play the game with the numbers between 100 and 200. Write a paragraph describing the strategies you used when playing the game. What strategy do you consider to be the most successful? least successful?
2. Design another game that could be played using this program or a modification of the program. A challenging game could involve using friendly (amicable) numbers.

More Than Graphs, Revised Edition • ©2004 Key Curriculum Press

Playing the Numbers

Objective:	To estimate the sum of the factors of a given number, and also predict whether or not the number is a prime number
Materials needed:	TI-73, TI-82, TI-83, or TI-83 Plus graphing calculator
Appropriate Level:	Algebra and pre-algebra
Time involved:	One or two class periods
Preparation:	Prior introduction to divisibility tests would be desirable

This activity gives students the opportunity to develop their estimation and mental computation skills while playing a game. Students should develop strategies for making intelligent guesses concerning the sum of the factors of a number. They should also notice that the sum of the factors of a prime number is always 1 (since the number itself is not included in the sum). Using divisibility tests can help students make their predictions.

They will also learn how to use a LIST function to find their total score. By making a list of all the scores after all games have been completed, the class can determine the mean, median, and mode of the scores. After looking at these indicators, have them develop criteria for determining great estimators, good estimators, or those who need more practice.

Number	<	>	=
1	✔		
2	✔		
3	✔		
4	✔		
5	✔		
6			✔
7	✔		
8	✔		
9	✔		
10	✔		
11	✔		
12		✔	
13	✔		
14	✔		
15	✔		
16	✔		
17	✔		
18		✔	
19	✔		
20		✔	
21	✔		
22	✔		
23	✔		
24		✔	
25	✔		
	20	4	1

Number	<	>	=
26	✔		
27	✔		
28			✔
29	✔		
30		✔	
31	✔		
32	✔		
33	✔		
34	✔		
35	✔		
36		✔	
37	✔		
38	✔		
39	✔		
40		✔	
41	✔		
42		✔	
43	✔		
44	✔		
45	✔		
46	✔		
47	✔		
48		✔	
49	✔		
50	✔		
	19	5	1

More Than Graphs, Revised Edition • ©2004 Key Curriculum Press

Number	<	>	=
51	✔		
52	✔		
53	✔		
54		✔	
55	✔		
56		✔	
57	✔		
58	✔		
59	✔		
60		✔	
61	✔		
62	✔		
63	✔		
64	✔		
65	✔		
66		✔	
67	✔		
68	✔		
69	✔		
70		✔	
71	✔		
72		✔	
73	✔		
74	✔		
75	✔		
	19	6	0

Number	<	>	=
76	✔		
77	✔		
78		✔	
79	✔		
80		✔	
81	✔		
82	✔		
83	✔		
84		✔	
85	✔		
86	✔		
87	✔		
88		✔	
89	✔		
90		✔	
91	✔		
92	✔		
93	✔		
94	✔		
95	✔		
96		✔	
97	✔		
98	✔		
99	✔		
100		✔	
	18	7	0

Number	<	>	=
101	✔		
102		✔	
103	✔		
104		✔	
105	✔		
106	✔		
107	✔		
108		✔	
109	✔		
110	✔		
111	✔		
112		✔	
113	✔		
114		✔	
115	✔		
116	✔		
117	✔		
118	✔		
119	✔		
120		✔	
121	✔		
122	✔		
123	✔		
124	✔		
125	✔		
	19	6	0

Number	<	>	=
126			
127	✔		
128	✔	✔	
129	✔		
130	✔	✔	
131	✔		
132			
133	✔		
134	✔	✔	
135	✔		
136	✔		
137	✔		
138		✔	
139	✔		
140		✔	
141	✔		
142	✔		
143	✔		
144			
145	✔		
146	✔	✔	
147	✔		
148	✔		
149	✔		
150		✔	
	19	6	0

Number	<	>	=
151	✔		
152	✔		
153	✔		
154	✔		
155	✔		
156		✔	
157	✔		
158	✔		
159	✔		
160		✔	
161	✔		
162		✔	
163	✔		
164	✔		
165	✔		
166	✔		
167	✔		
168		✔	
169	✔		
170	✔		
171	✔		
172	✔		
173	✔		
174		✔	
175	✔		
	20	5	0

Number	<	>	=
176		✔	
177	✔		
178	✔		
179	✔		
180		✔	
181	✔		
182	✔		
183	✔		
184	✔		
185	✔		
186		✔	
187	✔		
188	✔		
189	✔		
190	✔		
191	✔		
192		✔	
193	✔		
194	✔		
195	✔		
196		✔	
197	✔		
198		✔	
199	✔		
200		✔	
	18	7	0

Shape Shifter

Using Parametric Equations to Create Geometric Shapes

Setting the Stage

You can use parametric equations and your calculator to create impressive pictures ranging from circles and polygons to stars and ellipses. Parametric equations are equations in which a parameter or variable, usually t, changes over time. As t varies, so do the functions of t, which we will call X1T and Y1T. In this activity, you will be experimenting with the parametric equations X1T = $3 \cos t$ and Y1T = $3 \sin t$ to create shapes on your calculator.

The Activity

The key to creating just the right picture is to choose your window settings carefully. To start out, set each screen as shown below. (Use 2nd [FORMAT] to turn the axes off.)

TI-82/TI-83

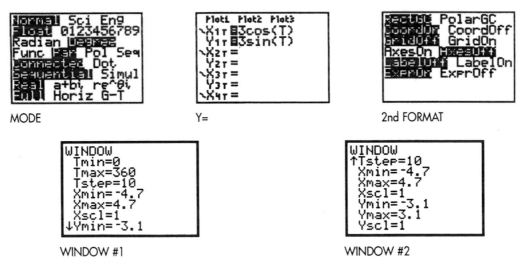

MODE

Y=

2nd FORMAT

WINDOW #1

WINDOW #2

Press GRAPH and you should see what appears to be a circle.

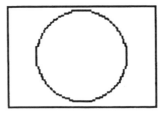

By changing one of the WINDOW settings, you can make the circle change to a diagonal square. Experiment with different settings to make this happen.

Record your WINDOW settings here.

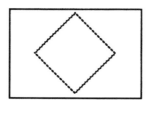

WINDOW	FORMAT
Tmin = _____	
Tmax = _____	
Tstep = _____	
Xmin = _____	
Xmax = _____	
Xscl = _____	
Ymin = _____	
Ymax = _____	
Yscl = _____	

By changing two more WINDOW settings, you can get this picture. Experiment and find WINDOW settings that work.

Record your WINDOW settings here.

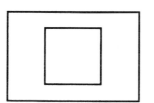

WINDOW	FORMAT
Tmin = _____	
Tmax = _____	
Tstep = _____	
Xmin = _____	
Xmax = _____	
Xscl = _____	
Ymin = _____	
Ymax = _____	
Yscl = _____	

Practice Problems

Change one or two WINDOW settings to create each shape. Record the WINDOW settings you used. Compare your results with the results of others. Is there more than one way to draw each picture?

1. an equilateral triangle

```
WINDOW        FORMAT
  Tmin = _____
  Tmax = _____
  Tstep = _____
  Xmin = _____
  Xmax = _____
  Xscl = _____
  Ymin = _____
  Ymax = _____
  Yscl = _____
```

2. a hexagon

```
WINDOW        FORMAT
  Tmin = _____
  Tmax = _____
  Tstep = _____
  Xmin = _____
  Xmax = _____
  Xscl = _____
  Ymin = _____
  Ymax = _____
  Yscl = _____
```

3. an octagon

```
WINDOW        FORMAT
  Tmin = _____
  Tmax = _____
  Tstep = _____
  Xmin = _____
  Xmax = _____
  Xscl = _____
  Ymin = _____
  Ymax = _____
  Yscl = _____
```

4. a 5-pointed star

```
WINDOW        FORMAT
  Tmin = _____
  Tmax = _____
  Tstep = _____
  Xmin = _____
  Xmax = _____
  Xscl = _____
  Ymin = _____
  Ymax = _____
  Yscl = _____
```

5. an 8-pointed star

```
WINDOW        FORMAT
  Tmin = _____
  Tmax = _____
  Tstep = _____
  Xmin = _____
  Xmax = _____
  Xscl = _____
  Ymin = _____
  Ymax = _____
  Yscl = _____
```

6. an ellipse

```
WINDOW        FORMAT
  Tmin = _____
  Tmax = _____
  Tstep = _____
  Xmin = _____
  Xmax = _____
  Xscl = _____
  Ymin = _____
  Ymax = _____
  Yscl = _____
```

Extension Problems

1. Create an ellipse by changing the equations in the Y= menu. See if you can also rotate the ellipse.
2. Experiment by changing the equations in the Y= menu to see how many different kinds of pictures you can make.

More Than Graphs, Revised Edition • ©2004 Key Curriculum Press

Shape Shifter

Objective: To experiment with parametric equations to create geometric shapes
Materials needed: TI-82, TI-83, or TI-83 Plus graphing calculator
Appropriate level: Algebra and pre-algebra
Time involved: One hour or class period
Preparation: Familiarity with polygon terminology

Some helpful hints:

1. What appears to be a circle on the calculator screen is actually not a circle, but a polygon with 36 sides.

2. Tstep tells the calculator how often to recalculate a value.

In this lesson, students are faced with a series of challenges that have to do with the initial settings of their calculator. When each chal-lenge is successfully met, they are rewarded with a picture of the correct polygon on the screen. It's very open-ended, with a great deal of sharing and discovery. The key to many of the solutions is the Tstep settings. The number of times Tstep divides into Tmax determines the number of sides of the polygon. Change the values of k and l in $X1T = \sin(kt)$ and $Y1T = \cos(kt)$ to see how the two constants relate.

Solutions

Activity

(There is more than one possible solution.)

Diagonal Square	Tmin = 0	Tmax = 360	Tstep = 90
Level Square	Tmin = 45	Tmax = 405	Tstep = 90

Practice Problems

(There is more than one possible solution to each problem.)

1. Equilateral triangle	Tmin = 0	Tmax = 360	Tstep = 120
2. Hexagon	Tmin = 0	Tmax = 360	Tstep = 60
3. Octagon	Tmin = 0	Tmax = 360	Tstep = 45
4. 5-pointed star	Tmin = 0	Tmax = 720	Tstep = 144
5. 8-pointed star	Tmin = 0	Tmax = 1080	Tstep = 135

6. Ellipse   Change the Xmax or Xmin and/or the Ymax or Ymin. (This solution really just changes the proportion along one or both of the axes.)

Extension Problems

Answers will vary.

Editing Pythagoras

Applying the Distance Formula

Setting the Stage

An early mathematician, Pythagoras of Samos lived in the sixth century B.C. and founded a special and somewhat mystical order of mathematicians called the Pythagoreans. Today, however, he is much more renowned for the Pythagorean theorem, which was named after him because of his famous proof. Although this theorem has been credited to Pythagoras, there is some evidence that he may have learned it in Babylonia and Egypt, where he spent his youth. Some historians say that in the days of the Egyptian master builders, the ancient engineers would carry rope loops of knots on their belts. By stretching the ropes so there were intervals of 3, 4, and 5 on each side of the triangle, the engineers could create a 90-degree angle.

The Activity

The Pythagorean theorem says that the square of the longest side of a right triangle (c) can be found by adding the squares of the two shorter sides (a and b). This can be written in either of two ways:

If a triangle is a right triangle, $a^2 + b^2 = c^2$ or $c = \sqrt{a^2 + b^2}$.

The converse of the theorem states that if $a^2 + b^2 = c^2$, then the triangle is a right triangle.

The formula for finding the distance between any two points on a Cartesian plane is based on the Pythagorean theorem.

distance^2 = (difference in x-coordinates)^2 + (difference in y-coordinates)^2

To find the distance between $A = (6, 8)$ and $B = (12, 16)$ using the distance formula, enter the expression directly into your calculator.

To enter $\sqrt{(12-6)^2 + (16-8)^2}$, press ⟨ 2nd ⟩ [√] ((12 − 6) ⟨ x^2 ⟩ + (16 − 8) ⟨ x^2 ⟩) ⟨ ENTER ⟩. Try this now.

You should get 10, which means the two points are 10 units apart.

More Than Graphs, Revised Edition • ©2004 Key Curriculum Press

To repeat the process for another pair of points, you don't have to reenter the whole expression. Press ⌐2nd¬ [ENTRY], and the original expression will reappear. Now you can edit the expression using the right and left arrows, and the INS (insert) and DEL (delete) commands. Try editing the command to find the distance between C (9, 13) and D (−4, 5). Did you get 15.264433752?

Practice Problems

Find the distance between each pair of points.
1. (0, 0) and (−3, 4)
2. (1, 2) and (6, 14)
3. (8, 11) and (15, 35)
4. (3, 8) and (−5, −7)
5. (−2, 3) and (−1, 4)
6. (4, 1) and (−1, −3)
7. (−6, 3) and (1, −2)
8. The points (0, 0), (3, 1), and (−1, 1) form a triangle. Is it an isosceles triangle? Prove that it is or it isn't.
9. The points (−6, 2), (5, −1), and (4, 4) form a triangle. Is it a right triangle? Prove that it is or it isn't.
10. The vertices of a quadrilateral are (4, −3), (7, 10), (−8, 2), and (−1, −5). Find the length of each diagonal.
11. Find the perimeter of a triangle formed by the vertices (5, 7), (1, 10), and (−3, −8).

Extension Problems

1. In three-dimensional space you can extend the Pythagorean theorem to find the distance between any two points. The distance from the origin in space (0, 0, 0) to point (a, b, c) is given by the equation, distance = $\sqrt{a^2 + b^2 + c^2}$. What is the length of the segment between each point and the origin? (Hint: When squaring a negative number, you will need to use parentheses. To square −2, enter $(−2)^2$. Otherwise, the calculator will think you want to find the opposite of 2^2, which is −4.)
    a. (5, 9, 6)   b. (−2, 4, −7)   c. (4, −8, 12)
2. To find the distance between two points in space, you will need to modify the distance formula used for two points on a plane. The distance formula for space looks like this:
$$d = \sqrt{(x_2 - x_1)^2 + (y_2 - y_1)^2 + (z_2 - z_1)^2}$$
Use this formula to find the distance between each pair of points below.
    a. (4, −1, 5) and (7, 3, 7)
    b. (0, 4, 5) and (−6, 2, 8)
    c. (3, 0, 7) and (−1, 3, 7)
3. Write a calculator program that asks you to input the endpoint values for a segment and then calculates the length of the segment.

Editing Pythagoras

Objective: To use the Pythagorean theorem to draw conclusions
Materials needed: TI-73, TI-82, TI-83, or TI-83 Plus graphing calculator
Appropriate level: Algebra and pre-algebra
Time involved: One hour or class period
Preparation: An earlier introduction to the Pythagorean theorem is helpful

Although this lesson is basically computational in nature, it provides a good opportunity to introduce students to the meaning of function. Encourage students to use this feature, as it can be quite useful when working with complex expressions.

For students who are interested in programming, this lesson might be a good place for them to start. If a student, or students, does write a program, be sure to let them share it with the class.

Solutions

Practice Problems

1. 5 units
2. 13 units
3. 25 units
4. 17 units
5. ≈ 1.414 units
6. ≈ 6.403 units
7. ≈ 11.18 units
8. Two of the sides are 5 units long.
   Since two sides are equal, the triangle is isosceles.
9. $(\text{side } a)^2 = 26$
   $(\text{side } b)^2 = 104$
   $(\text{side } c)^2 = 130$
   Since $a^2 + b^2 = c^2$, the triangle is a right triangle.
10. The diagonals are 17 units and 13 units long.
11. The sides are 5 units, 18.439 units, and 17 units long,
    so perimeter = 40.439 units.

Extension Problems

1. a. ≈ 11.92 units   b. ≈ 8.31 units   c. ≈ 14.97 units
2. a. ≈ 5.385 units   b. 7 units   c. 5 units

More Than Graphs, Revised Edition • ©2004 Key Curriculum Press

Irrational Numbers

Determining an Approximate Value for an Irrational Number

Setting the Stage

The existence of irrational numbers was a startling discovery for the ancient mathematicians. They had believed that numbers consisted only of the whole numbers and of those fractions that could be expressed as the ratio of two whole numbers. These make up the family of numbers that is now called the *rational numbers*. Hippasus of Metapontum is credited with discovering numbers such as $\sqrt{2}$, which are not rational. At the time that Hippasus demonstrated this, the Pythagoreans are said to have been at sea. The story is that they threw Hippasus overboard for finding an element in the universe that disagreed with their beliefs about numbers. Although this story may not be historically accurate, it does say something about how difficult it was for these early mathematicians to accept the idea of irrational numbers. Irrational numbers continued to tease mathematicians. It was not until the Middle Ages that they were able to confirm that π and $\sqrt{10}$ did not have the same value. Mathematicians could not believe that two irrational numbers could be so near each other and yet be two separate numbers. Later it was discovered that there were many other types of irrational numbers such as e and $0.101001000100001. \ldots$

Even today irrational numbers seem mysterious. It is easy to model whole numbers and fractions. You have probably used fraction blocks and wedges of pies or pizza to grapple with fraction problems, but what does an irrational number look like? How do you get your hands on an irrational number so you can know and understand it?

Computers and algorithms can extend approximations to many decimal places, but early estimates of these values, which were very accurate, were done entirely by measurement. In one of the Extension Problems, you will use measurements to explore an irrational number, much the same way the ancient Greeks did.

The Activity

Is there a relationship between the length of a side and the length of a diagonal for a square? To find out you will need to draw four different-sized squares on your calculator screen. For each square, you will record the coordinates of the vertices and use the distance formula to calculate the length of the diagonal. Use the following WINDOW setting:

[0, 47, 5, 0, 31, 5]

Select GridOn in the WINDOW FORMAT screen. (Press [2nd] [FORMAT] GridOn on the TI-73 and TI-83.) Press [2nd] [DRAW] [2] ([DRAW] [2] on the TI-73). Draw a square. Record the vertices on the diagram, and calculate the length of the diagonal. Do this for three more squares.

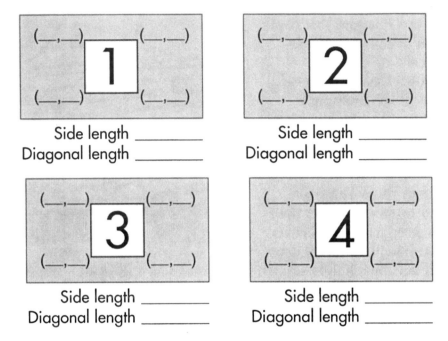

Side length _____
Diagonal length _____

Side length _____
Diagonal length _____

Side length _____
Diagonal length _____

Side length _____
Diagonal length _____

Press [STAT] and select EDIT ([LIST] on the TI-73). Enter the side lengths in L1 and the diagonal lengths in L2, and use STAT PLOT to plot the points. (Be sure to select appropriate WINDOW values.) What do you notice about these points? Do they appear to lie on a line?

Find the regression equation. Use [STAT] CALC [5] for the TI-82; [STAT] CALC [4] for the TI-83; [2nd] [STAT] CALC [5] for the TI-73.

Regression equation: $y = $ _____

Note: You may get a strange-looking number for the b-value. If the calculator gives you a number that looks like 7.5E−13, this means 0.00000000000075, which is very close to zero. In fact, it is sometimes the way the calculator expresses zero because of rounding errors.

When the b-value is zero, the linear equation is called a **direct variation**. This means that it is the equation of a line that passes through the origin. A direct variation is an equation that looks like $y = kx$, where k is called the **constant of variation**. In this situation the constant of variation is equal to the ratio L2/L1, which is the ratio of the diagonal length to the side length for the squares you drew. What is this ratio? _____

Now experiment with the $\sqrt{}$ function, which is (2nd) [$\sqrt{}$] on your calculator, to figure out which irrational number seems to be closest to this ratio. Use it to complete the next sentence.

The ratio of the diagonal to the side of a square is _____.

Practice Problems

1. Repeat the activity above but with rectangles. Draw four different-sized rectangles. In each rectangle the ratio of the short side to the long side should be 1:2. You may want to use graph paper to help you plan your rectangles.

	Short Side Length	Diagonal Length
Rectangle 1		
Rectangle 2		
Rectangle 3		
Rectangle 4		

Calculate the length of the short side and diagonal of each rectangle, and record the lengths in the table.

Press (STAT) and select EDIT ((LIST) on the TI-73). Enter the side lengths in L1 and the diagonal lengths in L2, and calculate the linear regression.
Regression equation: $y =$ _____
Is the equation a direct variation? _____
If so, what is the constant of variation? _____

Experiment again with the $\sqrt{}$ function to figure out which irrational number this ratio equals, and complete the next sentence.
In a rectangle in which the long side is _____ times as long as the short side, the ratio of the diagonal to the short side is _____.

2. Repeat Problem 1 for a rectangle in which the ratio of the short side to the long side is 1:3.
3. Repeat Problem 1 for a right triangle in which the ratio of the short side to the long side is 1:4.

Extension Problems

1. Work with a partner to compare the length of the side of an equilateral triangle to the length of its altitude. Use a large compass or a piece of string to construct four different-sized equilateral triangles on butcher paper or newspaper. You may find it helpful to do this on a background of squares. Measure both the base and altitude of each triangle, and record your measurements in the table below.

   Enter the lengths of the bases in L1, and the lengths of the altitudes in L3. The relationship in an equilateral triangle is easier to see if you compare half the length of the base to the altitude, so in L2, enter 0.5L1. To do this, place the cursor so it highlights L2 and press 0.5 [2nd] [L1] [ENTER]. (On the TI-73, L1 is found by pressing [2nd] [STAT] [1].)

Base (cm)	½ Base (cm)	Altitude (cm)

   To calculate the regression equation, follow the usual steps and then when the calculator displays LinReg($ax + b$) enter L1, L2 and press [ENTER].
   $y =$ _____
   What is the constant of variation? _____
   Experiment to determine which irrational number this constant approximates and use it to complete the sentence:

   > In an equilateral triangle, the ratio of one-half the length of a side to the length of the altitude is _____.

2. Explain how this picture demonstrates that $\sqrt{2} \cdot \sqrt{32} = \sqrt{64} = 8$. Design two more visual models to confirm the multiplication property of irrationals.

More Than Graphs, Revised Edition • ©2004 Key Curriculum Press

Irrational Numbers

Objective: To determine an approximate value for irrational numbers by measurement
Materials needed: TI-73, TI-82, TI-83, or TI-83 Plus graphing calculator
Appropriate level: Algebra and pre-algebra
Time involved: One hour or class period
Preparation: Some discussion of radicals and irrational numbers

One of the truths about mathematics, whether accepted as gospel or discovered by personal insight, is that to really understand math a person has to see it. Hearing about it or reading about it is not the same as seeing it happen. In this unit, I tried to help the students visualize a series of irrationals by studying the diagonals of different rectangles and the hypotenuses of right triangles.

In each case, the length of the diagonal, or hypotenuse, could be confirmed by using the Pythagorean theorem, but for some reason that doesn't usually seem to occur to the students. The irrational number, represented by the ratio of the diagonal length to the side length, or the ratio of y to x in the regression equation, is the constant in the direct variation equation that results from finding the regression line. This is also the slope of the line of regression.

You could also do this activity by asking students to draw large geometric figures and then measure the appropriate lengths. In this case, the more measurements that are taken, the closer the ratio or slope should be to the value of the irrational number, which represents the constant of variation. Greater accuracy should also be achieved with larger shapes, which is why instead of graph paper, you should consider using configurations of floor tiles or figures drawn on butcher paper or newspaper.

The altitude of the equilateral triangle was the problem that seemed to provoke the greatest intrigue. It would be helpful if the students have done some compass and straightedge constructions before attempting that one.

Solutions

Practice Problems

1. The constant of variation should be approximately $\sqrt{5}$.
2. The constant of variation should be approximately $\sqrt{10}$.
3. The constant of variation should be approximately $\sqrt{17}$.

Extension Problems

1. The constant of variation should be $\frac{2}{\sqrt{3}}$.

2. The length of the short side of the rectangle is $\sqrt{1^2 + 1^2} = \sqrt{2}$. The length of the long side is $\sqrt{4^2 + 4^2} = \sqrt{32}$. Therefore, the area of the rectangle is $\sqrt{2} \cdot \sqrt{32} = \sqrt{64} = 8$.

The Big Bouncer
Creating a Mathematical Model

Setting the Stage

If you drop a golf ball from the top of the Empire State Building in New York City, how many times will it bounce?

There are two questions you would need to answer before trying to solve this problem. The first is, "How tall is the Empire State Building?" A speedy trip to the almanac would give you an answer of 1250 feet. The next question is, "How high can a golf ball bounce?" That answer is entirely dependent on the height from which you drop it. Since New Yorkers frown upon tourists throwing objects off the Empire State Building onto their city streets, a simulation would seem to be the appropriate means to solve this problem.

The Activity

To make predictions about the behavior of a golf ball, you need to observe the behavior of the ball in a very controlled environment. In this experiment, you will drop a standard golf ball from a height of 100 cm and measure the highest point of its return bounce. This will tell you the ball's resiliency factor.

If the ball bounced to a height of 50 cm, that would indicate a resiliency of 0.5. You can use the calculator to find out how many times the ball will bounce and how high it will bounce each time.

Clear the screen, enter the value of 100, and press `ENTER`.
Type .5 · `2nd` [`ANS`] to see the height of the next bounce.
Press `ENTER` repeatedly to see the height of each successive bounce.

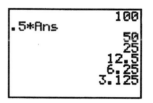

The golf ball in this example with a resiliency factor of 0.5 would return to a height of approximately 3.125 cm on the fifth bounce and about 1 mm on the tenth bounce.

Now conduct your own experiment. Release a golf ball from a height of 1 m and record the return height of its rebound.

     Return height _____

Divide this return height by the initial height to get the resiliency factor.

     Resiliency factor _____

Use your calculator and the resiliency factor to complete this table.

Bounce Number	Height of Bounce
1	
2	
3	
4	
5	
6	
7	

This table of bounce heights can be described by a *recursive function*. The word *recursive* comes from the word *recur*, which means to occur again. In a recursive function, each successive entry is found by multiplying or adding something to the previous entry. If b_n is the height of the nth bounce, b_{n+1} is the height of the next bounce, and r is the resiliency factor, then you can define the height of bounces by this recursive function:

$$b_1 = 100$$
$$b_{n+1} = r \cdot b_n$$

Computers and calculators are very good for simulating recursive functions. Here is a program that will simulate the height of a bouncing ball. You get to input the height and the resiliency factor. Input one of these programs in your calculator.

TI-82/TI-83 Program
```
PROGRAM:BOUNCER
ClrHome
Disp "INITIAL HEIGHT"
Input H
Disp "RESILIENCY FCTR"
Input R
0→B
ClrHome
Disp "PRESS ENTER TO"
Disp "SEE MORE VALUES."
Disp " "
Disp "BOUNCE AND","HEIGHT"
Lbl 1
B+1→B
H*R→H
Disp B,H
Pause
Goto 1
```

TI-73 Program
```
PROGRAM:BOUNCER
ClrScreen
Disp "INITIAL HEIGHT"
Input H
Disp "RESILIENCY FCTR"
Input R
0→B
ClrScreen
Disp "PRESS ENTER TO"
Disp "SEE MORE VALUES."
Disp " "
Disp "BOUNCE AND","HEIGHT"
Lbl 1
B+1→B
H*R→H
Disp B,H
Pause
Goto 1
```

Press ⌈ON⌉ and select Quit to stop the program. Press ⌈ENTER⌉ to run the program again.

Practice Problems

1. Simulate dropping your golf ball off of the Empire State Building, and record your results in the table.

   How many bounces are there before the rebound height is less than 1 m?_____

Bounce Number	Height
1	
2	
3	
4	
5	
6	
7	
8	
9	
10	

Bounce Number	Height
11	
12	
13	
14	
15	
16	
17	
18	
19	
20	

   How many times does the ball bounce before it would appear not to bounce any more? _____

   Do you think this is a realistic model? _____ Why or why not?

2. a. Find the resiliency factor of a super ball. Resiliency factor _____

   b. Run BOUNCER to simulate dropping this ball from two different heights, such as from the roof of the school or the top of a fire department's snorkel truck.

Super Ball	Dropped From ------	Dropped From ------
Bounce Number	Height of Bounce	Height of Bounce
1		
2		
3		
4		
5		
6		
7		

3. a. Find the resiliency factor of a basketball. Resiliency factor _____
   b. Run BOUNCER to simulate dropping this ball from two different heights, such as from the roof of the school or the top of a fire department's snorkel truck.

Basketball	Dropped From ‑ ‑ ‑ ‑ ‑ ‑ ‑ ‑	Dropped From ‑ ‑ ‑ ‑ ‑ ‑ ‑ ‑
Bounce Number	Height of Bounce	Height of Bounce
1		
2		
3		
4		
5		
6		
7		

Extension Problems (For the TI-82 and TI-83)

Begin Graphing the Rebound Heights (TI-82)

Your calculator can graph bouncing balls as sequences. To do this, press [MODE] and highlight Seq for sequence.

```
Normal Sci Eng
Float 0123456789
Radian Degree
Func Par Pol Seq
Connected Dot
Sequential Simul
FullScreen Split
```

Now when you press [WINDOW], you will see a sequence window. To graph the rebound heights of a golf ball with a resiliency factor of 0.5, bouncing from an initial height of 100 cm, enter these WINDOW settings:

```
WINDOW FORMAT
 UnStart=100
 VnStart=0
 nStart=0
 nMin=0
 nMax=50
 Xmin=0
↓Xmax=20
```

```
WINDOW FORMAT
 nMax=50
 Xmin=0
 Xmax=20
 Xscl=1
 Ymin=0
 Ymax=100
 Yscl=10
```

Press [Y=] and set Un = Un–1 • .5. This makes each new value of Un equal to 0.5 times the previous value (Un–1).

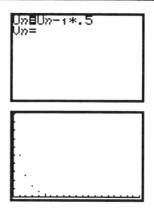

You don't need to enter anything in Vn.

Press [MODE] and change from Connected to Dot. Press [GRAPH] to see the heights of successive bounces.

Begin Graphing the Rebound Heights (TI-83)

The TI-83 calculator can also graph bouncing balls as sequences, but the procedures are a bit different. To do this, press [MODE], highlight Sequential, and change Connected to Dot. Use [2nd] [FORMAT] to make the default settings active.

MODE

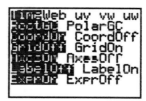

2nd FORMAT

When you press [WINDOW], you will also see a sequence window. To graph the rebound heights of a golf ball with a resiliency factor of 0.5, bouncing from an initial height of 100 cm, enter these WINDOW settings. This will display the decay of the bounce curve through the first 20 bounces.

```
WINDOW
 nMin=0
 nMax=20
 PlotStart=1
 PlotStep=1
 Xmin=0
 Xmax=20
↓Xscl=1
```

```
WINDOW
↑PlotStep=1
 Xmin=0
 Xmax=20
 Xscl=1
 Ymin=0
 Ymax=100
 Yscl=5∎
```

Press [Y=] and set un = .5u(n – 1), making each u(n) half of the previous value. Set u(nMin) = 100. Obtain u by pressing [2nd] [u], the second function of the [7] key. Obtain n by pressing the [X,T,θ,n] key. There is no v(n) or w(n) unless you want to graph several balls at once.

Press (GRAPH) to see the heights of successive bounces.

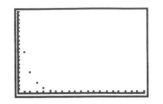

Push (2nd) [TABLE] to see a table showing the height of each successive bounce. The (TRACE) key may be helpful. You can see from the table that the rebound height of the golf ball drops below 0.5 cm after eight bounces. Values smaller than this are too suspect and subject to error to be credible. Eight bounces would be a reasonable predicted value for a ball that was dropped from a height of 1 m. Test this prediction.

1. Enter the WINDOW settings you would use to model dropping your golf ball off of the top of the Empire State Building.
   Graph the results.

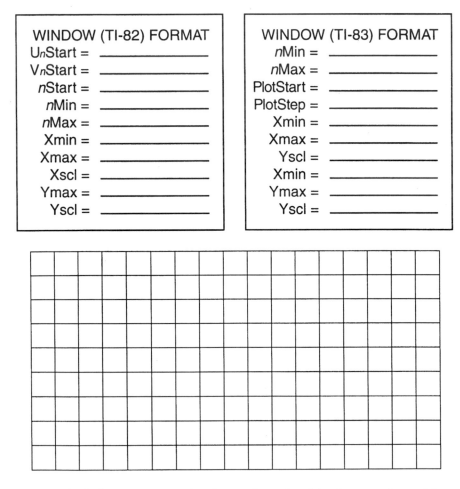

WINDOW (TI-82) FORMAT
UnStart = _____
VnStart = _____
nStart = _____
nMin = _____
nMax = _____
Xmin = _____
Xmax = _____
Xscl = _____
Ymax = _____
Yscl = _____

WINDOW (TI-83) FORMAT
nMin = _____
nMax = _____
PlotStart = _____
PlotStep = _____
Xmin = _____
Xmax = _____
Yscl = _____
Xmin = _____
Ymax = _____
Yscl = _____

2. Would dropping a ball from twice as high result in double the number of bounces? How many more should you expect to see? Use graphs and tables to explain your answer.

More Than Graphs, Revised Edition • ©2004 Key Curriculum Press

The Big Bouncer

Objective:	To use the results of collected data to design a mathematical model for a simulation
Materials needed:	TI-73, TI-82, TI-83, TI-83 Plus graphing calculator (Extension, TI-82 and TI-83 only), meter stick, several balls (tennis, ping-pong, super ball, baseball, golf ball, etc.)
Appropriate level:	Algebra and pre-algebra
Time involved:	One hour or class period
Preparation:	Find an open space away from breakable objects

The Big Bouncer does not present a lot of complicated mathematical concepts. It is a fairly simple introduction to the idea of a recursive function and to the efficiency of the calculator in generating the terms of a geometric sequence. The Extension Problems let students see the graph of the rebound heights.

This experiment can be a springboard for other discussions. It's a good place to introduce Galileo's gravity experiments, which he did by dropping two spheres off the Leaning Tower of Pisa. It's also a good place to develop the concept of **iteration**, since the output of each computation is the input for the next one.

Another interesting discussion can evolve if you ask students to try to guess, just from squeezing them, which of two balls will bounce higher, and then dropping both balls to test their predictions.

Solutions

Practice Problems

Answers will vary.

Extension Problems

Answers will vary.

Canoe Leapfrog

Using Calculator Regressions to Find Patterns

Setting the Stage

Ten people are floating down a river in a very large canoe with eleven seats. The seat in the center of the canoe is empty. The five men in front want to change seats and sit in the back of the canoe, and the five women in the back want to move to the front of the canoe. Anyone may move from their seat to the next empty seat, or they may carefully step over one person without capsizing the canoe. What is the minimum number of moves it will take for the five men in the front to exchange seats with the five women in the back?

M M M M   W W W W W

You can solve this problem using a variety of problem-solving strategies like solving a simpler problem, acting it out, making a diagram, and looking for patterns. Your calculator will also help you to find a mathematical model.

The Activity

A canoe with a middle seat and no passengers would be a simple problem to solve, but not particularly interesting. A little more challenging is a canoe with three seats and one pair of passengers. A person sits in each end with an empty seat in the middle. How many moves would it require for the two people to change seats?

Change the situation to two pairs of people and five seats. Remember that the middle one is always empty. What is the minimum number of moves now?

Repeat this process for three pairs, and record the number of moves in the table.

Store this data as a pair of lists in the STAT section of the calculator. Enter the number of pairs in L1 and the corresponding number of moves in L2. You can now study and plot this data using the STAT PLOT feature of your calculator.

In previous activities, you used the LinReg feature of your calculator to find an equation for y in terms of x. Use LinReg to find the equation of best fit for this data.

Linear seating formula: _____

Pairs of People	Moves Needed to Change Seats
0	
1	
2	
3	

Because the data in your table represents actual values rather than experimental data, you would like to be able to find a model that fits the points exactly. How well does this equation fit the points? Check to see if the points in your table satisfy the linear regression equation by substituting them into the equation. Does the equation fit the points? _____

TI calculators are able to build tables showing x- and y-values when you have a function listed in Y=. Enter the linear equation you found above into Y1. Press [2nd] [TblSet]. Enter a minimum value for x (TblMin on the TI-82 and TblStart on the TI-73 and TI-83) and the increment you want to use when counting by x (ΔTbl). Then press [2nd] [TABLE] to look at a table of values.

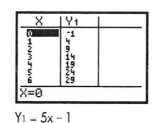

Y1 – 5x – 1

You can see that although the y-values are close to those in the table you completed, this linear equation does not fit the data exactly.

You can also see that the equation doesn't fit the points graphically. Use STAT PLOT to make a scatter plot of L1 and L2. Then enter the equation in Y= and press [GRAPH]. The result is the equation of the line on top of the points. Does the line pass through the points? _____

Press [STAT] and choose CALC [2nd] [STAT] (CALC on the TI-73). You will notice that there are several other regression functions that your calculator can find. Experiment to find an equation that *exactly* matches the table of data you created. Use the CATALOG feature to make certain that the calculator is set for DiagnosticOn.

Check the fit graphically and by looking at a table of values on your calculator.

Record the equation you found: $y =$ _____

Note: Be aware that sometimes calculators make very small errors because of the binary algorithms they use. Occasionally a value such as $^-3\text{E}^-13$ appears when you are expecting or hoping for zero. This is actually equal to $^-0.0000000000003$ and is essentially zero.

Use the equation to find the minimum number of moves necessary for all five couples to switch seats. _____

Practice Problems

1. Polynesians, early inhabitants of islands in the South Pacific, used very large canoes to travel from island to island. Some of these canoes were large enough to seat as many as 17 people. On ceremonial occasions or for very long trips, two of these canoes would be lashed together with a platform between them. If 8 men and 8 women were in such a 17-person canoe with one empty seat in the center, how many moves would it take for all the people in the back to change seats with all the people in the front?

2. Find an equation that exactly fits each table of values. Complete the table for the missing *x*- and *y*-values.

a.

x	y
0	−1
1	2
2	11
3	26
7	
12	
	587

b.

x	y
0	5
1	5
2	13
3	41
10	
15	
	13001

Extension Problem

Towers of Hanoi

The Towers of Hanoi is a famous puzzle, and it gives rise to a similar problem. In the Towers of Hanoi, three poles are in a line. On one of the poles, eight different-sized disks, each with a hole in the center, are stacked in order of size with the largest disk on the bottom. The object of the puzzle is to transfer the disks from the pole on one end to the pole on the other end with a minimum number of moves. A move consists of moving a disk to an adjacent pole or of leaping one disk over another. A larger disk is never allowed to rest on top of a smaller one. What is the minimum number of moves necessary to transfer a stack of eight disks? Use a quarter, a nickel, a penny, and a dime to study simpler cases with a smaller number of disks.

Canoe Leapfrog

Objective:	To use different built-in calculator regressions to solve pattern problems
Materials needed:	TI-73, TI-82, TI-83, or TI-83 Plus graphing calculator, possibly markers for modeling
Appropriate level:	Algebra and pre-algebra
Time involved:	One hour or class period
Preparation:	None

In this activity, students use a variety of problem-solving strategies including solving a simpler problem, acting it out, and looking for patterns. They also learn how to use various calculator functions to find and verify solutions. Students use the calculator table to examine x- and y values of a function, they learn how to use different built-in regression formulas to find equations, and they discover that not all patterns are linear.

Encourage students to use coins, beans, or some other manipulative to model the problem in the activity. For one pair, the seat exchange might look like this:

$$< A \: ! \: B >$$
$$< ! \: A \: B >$$
$$< B \: A \: ! >$$
$$< B \: ! \: A >$$

So the switch can be done in three moves.

For two pairs, the seat exchange might look like this:

$$< A \: A \: ! \: B \: B >$$
$$< A \: ! \: A \: B \: B >$$
$$< A \: B \: A \: ! \: B >$$
$$< A \: B \: A \: B \: ! >$$
$$< A \: B \: ! \: B \: A >$$
$$< ! \: B \: A \: B \: A >$$
$$< B \: ! \: A \: B \: A >$$
$$< B \: B \: A \: ! \: A >$$
$$< B \: B \: ! \: A \: A >$$

So this switch requires eight moves.

The completed table of values looks like this:

Pairs of People	Moves Needed to Change Seats
0	0
1	3
2	8
3	15

Using this set of data points, the LinReg equation is $y = 5x - 1$. The regression equation that fits exactly is found using QuadReg and is $y = x^2 + 2x$.

Solutions

Practice Problems

1. It would take 72 moves.

2a.

x	y
7	146
12	431
14	587

b.

x	y
10	1805
15	6305
19	13001

Extension Problem

For the Towers of Hanoi, the number of moves for the 8 disks is $2^8 - 1 = 255$.

Pick's Theorem

Looking for Patterns and Finding Equations

Setting the Stage

Can you see a relationship between the area, the number of points in the interior, and the number of points on the boundary of a polygon drawn on square dot paper? A Czechoslovakian mathematician by the name of Georg Pick, who was a colleague of Albert Einstein, did. In this activity, you'll replicate his discovery.

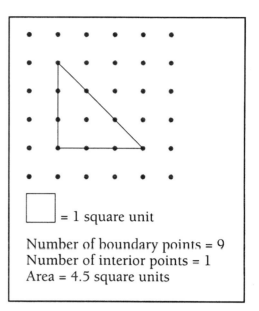

☐ = 1 square unit

Number of boundary points = 9
Number of interior points = 1
Area = 4.5 square units

The Activity

In order to find this relationship, you will need to collect some data. Start by drawing figures that each have three boundary points and the given number of interior points so you can complete the table on the next page. Then do the same thing for four boundary points and for five boundary points. Complete as many entries as you need to in each table until you discover the pattern. (If you really get stuck, there's a hint on the next page. But try not to look at it until you've put some effort into solving the problem.)

A name for your theorem? You pick.

3 Boundary Points	
Number of Interior Points	Area (Sq Units)
0	
1	
2	
3	
4	
5	
6	
7	

4 Boundary Points	
Number of Interior Points	Area (Sq Units)
0	
1	
2	
3	
4	
5	
6	
7	

5 Boundary Points	
Number of Interior Points	Area (Sq Units)
0	
1	
2	
3	
4	
5	
6	
7	

You can draw the figures on square grid dot paper, or without too much effort, you can draw them on your calculator. Select GridOn and AxesOff (2nd [FORMAT] on the TI-73 and TI-83; WINDOW FORMAT on the TI-82). Use the following WINDOW settings:

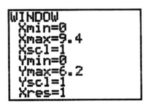

On the TI-73, there is also a ΔX, but this is calculated by the calculator and not set by you. Press GRAPH and select Line in the DRAW menu. Use the free-moving cursor to create your polygon. If you press ENTER twice each time you get to a vertex of your polygon, you won't have to reselect the LINE function every time you start to draw a new side.

Find the relationship between the area and the number of interior points for each table. If you don't see a pattern, you can use your calculator, and enter the number of interior points in L1 and the area number in L2. Use one of the calculator regressions to find an equation that fits the data in each table. Use I to represent the number of interior points.

3-point formula
$A = I +$ _____

4-point formula
$A = I +$ _____

5-point formula
$A = I +$ _____

After you find the three equations, you are ready to discover the general formula that relates the area, the number of interior points, and the number of boundary points for any polygon, using B to represent the number of boundary points. Be sure to check your formula using the data you already collected to make sure it works.

$A =$ _____

More Than Graphs, Revised Edition • ©2004 Key Curriculum Press

Hints: Here is a figure with 3 boundary points and 3 interior points:

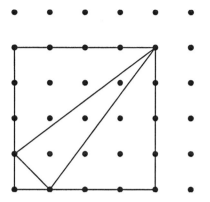

Do you see that by just moving one point, the 3-boundary-point figure can also become several different isosceles triangles with 0, 1, 2, or 4 interior points?

You can compute its area by surrounding the triangle with a square, computing the area of the square, and subtracting the areas of the three right triangles.

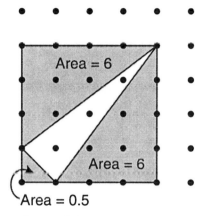

Area of the square = 16 square units
Area of the inside triangle = 16 − 6 − 6 − 0.5 + 3.5 square units

Practice Problem

Create at least three irregular-shaped polygons of your own. Test each polygon to see if Pick's theorem still works.

Extension Problem

Leonhard Euler was an incredibly productive eighteenth-century mathematician and physicist. He was born near Basel, Switzerland, and began publishing mathematics papers when he was eighteen. He spent many years working for Frederick the Great of Berlin and then later

Catherine the Great of Russia. He had a wide variety of interests both mathematical and otherwise. His memory was so phenomenal that he could do mathematical computations in his head, which most mathematicians would have trouble doing on paper. In addition to his academic interests, Euler had a rich family life. He was married and had thirteen children. He was very involved in his family and enjoyed making up scientific games for his children and grandchildren.

In this Extension you will explore Euler's formula for polyhedra. This formula relates the vertices, edges, and surfaces of solid polyhedra. It is actually only one of the many formulas with Euler's name on it!

Build some polyhedra, using soda straws and string or modeling clay and toothpicks. Record the number of vertices, surfaces, and edges in the table below.

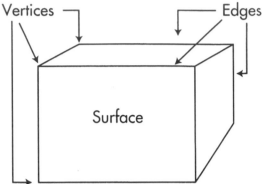

Sketch Your Polyhedron	Number of Vertices	Number of Surfaces	Number of Edges

Find a formula that will relate the number of vertices, surfaces, and edges.

If you're having trouble finding the formula, enter the values for the edges in L1, the surfaces in L2, and the edges in L4. Got it yet? No? Experiment using different operations with L1 and L2. For example, if you want to divide L1 by L2, move the cursor so it's on top of L3, then enter L1/L2 and press ⟮ENTER⟯. The calculator will compute the entire list of values for you all at once. You can then compare the list of values you have in L4 to the calculated values in L3.

Can you see the pattern yet?

$E =$ _____

Pick's Theorem

      Objective: To find a formula relating area, the number of points on the border, and the number of interior points for a polygon drawn on square grid dot paper

Materials needed: TI-73, TI-82, TI-83, or TI-83 Plus graphing calculator; graph or dot paper; soda straws and string, modeling clay and toothpicks, or some other materials for building polyhedra for the Extension

Appropriate level: Algebra and pre-algebra

  Time involved: Two hours or class periods, with the Extension

    Preparation: Experience with geoboards

In this activity students will link the idea of functions with the study of plane figures in geometry by collecting data and observing the relationship between border points, interior points, and area. In each case, by holding the boundary points constant it is possible to see a relationship between interior points and area of a polygon.

❏ For three boundary points, the formula is $A = I + 0.5$.

❏ For four boundary points, the formula is $A = I + 1$.

❏ For five boundary points, the formula is $A = I + 1.5$.

By studying the changing relationship between the constants in the three formulas, students may hypothesize and test Pick's theorem. It states $A = I + 0.5 (B - 2)$.

In the Extension, students do similar analysis in which they find a relationship between the number of edges, vertices, and surfaces for polyhedra.

Solutions

Practice Problem

Answers will vary.

Extension Problem

Euler's theorem states $E = V + S - 2$.

Modeling Jury Verdicts

STAT PROB

Using the Graphing Calculator to Simulate Courtroom Drama

Setting the Stage

In three different criminal cases, *Johnson v. Louisiana* (1972), *Williams v. Florida* (1970), and *Apodoca v. Oregon* (1972), the defendants argued that their rights to a fair trial had been abridged by having juries of fewer than twelve members. In the latter two cases, the defendants further claimed that their rights had been compromised by having been convicted by non-unanimous verdicts. In each of these cases, the states chose to use mathematical models to show that the likelihood of conviction over acquittal was not increased by altering the size of the jury or by allowing a non-unanimous verdict.

The Activity

Simulating Unanimous Verdicts

In any trial there is a possibility that the jury will vote for conviction or acquittal on the first ballot. After this point, there is a very subjective process of discussion and persuasion among jurors until a verdict is reached. In some cases it becomes clearly apparent that it will not be possible to reach any type of consensus, in which case there is a hung jury. If you can assign a probability that a typical juror will vote for conviction on the first ballot, then you can determine the probability that the jury as a whole will vote for conviction on the first ballot. If, for example, you assign a probability of 0.9 that any randomly picked juror will vote for conviction, then you can assume that this same probability holds for any juror. To determine the probability that the jury as a whole will vote for conviction, multiply the probabilities for all of the jurors. Thus, if there are twelve jurors, the probability that they will all vote for conviction on the first ballot is

$$0.9 \times 0.9 \times 0.9 \times 0.9 \times 0.9 \times 0.9 \times 0.9 \times 0.9 \times 0.9 \times 0.9 \times 0.9 \times 0.9 = (0.9)^{12}$$
$$= 0.28, \text{ or } 28\%$$

If the probability that a juror will vote for conviction is 0.9, then the probability that he or she will vote for acquittal is 0.1 $(1 - 0.9 = 0.1)$. You can compute the probability that all jurors will vote for acquittal in the same manner.

$$0.1 \times 0.1 \times 0.1 \times 0.1 \times 0.1 \times 0.1 \times 0.1 \times 0.1 \times 0.1 \times 0.1 \times 0.1 \times 0.1 = (0.1)^{12}$$
$$= 0.000000000001, \text{ or } 0.0000000001\%$$

More Than Graphs, Revised Edition • ©2004 Key Curriculum Press

Practice Problems

1. Fill in the table with the likelihood of conviction or acquittal on the first ballot, based on the different jury sizes and the given probability of conviction.
   You can easily build this table using STAT EDIT (LIST on the TI-73). Store the values 10, 6, and 5 in list L1. These correspond to the number of jurors. Put the cursor at the top of list L2 and enter the formula $0.9 \wedge L1$. For list L3 enter the formula $0.1 \wedge L1$. The two lists, L2 and L3, will show, respectively, the probabilities for conviction and acquittal for the different-sized juries.

| Size of Jury | p(conviction) = 0.9 | | p(conviction) = 0.6 | | p(conviction) = 0.5 | |
	Conviction	Acquittal	Conviction	Acquittal	Conviction	Acquittal
10						
6						
5						

2. If there is an equal likelihood of conviction or acquittal (0.5 in each case), does the size of the jury actually favor one outcome over the other? Study the table and see if you can make a conclusion about how reducing the size of the jury might affect the likelihood of the outcome.

Extension Problems

Simulating Non-unanimous Verdicts

In the United Kingdom and other countries of the Commonwealth, a finding by a majority of jurors may be sufficient for conviction or acquittal. This has also been considered by district and circuit courts in the United States as a way to reduce the backlog of cases. It can be argued that even if a conviction is more likely than with a unanimous verdict, it's not favored. The likelihood of an acquittal is also more likely.

This process of studying the number of different possible outcomes is called the study of *combinatorics*. In this situation you want to study combinations in which there is exactly one dissension. If there is a jury with ten members, how many different combinations are there in which exactly one person disagrees with the rest of the jury? Can you figure this out by counting the different ways?

The way to write this using mathematical symbols is 10C1. This stands for the number of different ways that you can choose one object out of a group of ten. In the general case, nCr refers to the number of ways you can choose r things out of a group of n. On the calculator, you can find this function (nCr) in the MATH PRB menu.

Now enter 10 MATH PRB 3 9 ENTER to find 10C9. (This is 10 MATH PRB 4 9 ENTER on the TI-73.)

Notice that 10C1 also equals 10. Why is that?

Sample Problem

If the probability that each juror will vote for conviction is 0.9 and a consensus of at least five jurors is needed for a conviction, what is the likelihood of a first-round conviction with a six-person jury?

Solution

There are two situations to consider. In order to convict on the first round, either all of the jurors will vote for conviction, or five out of the six jurors will vote for conviction.

Let C represent a juror voting to convict and let A represent a juror voting to acquit.

Assume all the jurors vote for conviction. There is only one way that could occur:

CCCCCC $(0.9)^6 = 0.531441$, or about 53%

How many ways can five of the six jurors vote to convict? Use your calculator to find 6C5.

Did you find that there are 6 ways that this might occur? The different combinations can be represented as

CCCCCA	CCCCAC	CCCACC
CCACCC	CACCCC	ACCCCC

Since the probability of acquittal is equal to $1 - 0.9 = 0.1$, the probability of each of these possibilities is $(0.9)^5 \times (0.1) = 0.059049$, or about 6%. Since there are six ways that this might occur, multiply this answer by 6. The result is $6 \times 0.059049 = 0.354294$, or about 35%.

To find the probability that either all six jurors or five out of six jurors will vote for conviction, add the two probabilities.

$0.531441 + 0.354294 = 0.885735$, or about 89%

You might think that 0.9 seems to be too large for a conviction probability, but a district attorney's office will not press for a trial unless they feel the likelihood for a conviction, based on evidence or testimony, is very good.

1. In the previous example, the calculator told you that there are six possible arrangements in which exactly five out of six jurors will vote for a conviction (6C5 = 6). Explain why 6C1 also equals 6.
2. If the probability that any juror will vote for conviction is 0.8, find the probability that a defendant will be convicted by an eight-person jury if
   a. all eight jurors vote to convict.
   b. exactly seven out of eight jurors vote to convict.
   c. at least seven out of eight jurors vote to convict.
   d. at least seven out of eight jurors vote to acquit.
3. Use what you've learned in this activity to write a convincing argument for or against the idea of allowing non-unanimous jury verdicts. You may choose to write your argument from the perspective of the defense or the prosecution. You may also want to experiment with other conviction probabilities and other jury sizes.

More Than Graphs, Revised Edition • ©2004 Key Curriculum Press

Modeling Jury Verdicts

Objective: To simulate jury outcomes in a variety of situations
Materials needed: TI-73, TI-82, TI-83, or TI-83 Plus graphing calculator
Appropriate level: Algebra and pre-algebra
Time involved: Two hours or class periods with the Extension
Preparation: Limited knowledge of court processes and terminology

In this lesson, I tried to create a simulation of a real-life event that did not involve simply recording data from an experiment. This lesson can be adapted to any study of discrete math or probability. The basis for most of this lesson was a paper created by Bernard Grofman. I have taken some of the problems and excerpts from that article and directly applied them to the graphing calculator. If students are interested, they could do some research on this issue, or you could invite an attorney to speak to students about the complexities of jury selection.

I believe that using the power of the calculator to simulate real-life probabilities is something that can't be done often enough. Perhaps by forging these connections, we can break down the mistaken perception by students that understanding mathematics is relevant not only to a specific time during each school day but also to happenings in the real world.

Findings

In the cases of *Johnson v. Louisiana, Williams v. Florida,* and *Apodoca v. Oregon,* the United States Supreme Court ruled that jury size did not favor conviction over acquittal and that unanimous verdicts were not necessary to determine innocence or guilt. The convictions stood.

In later cases, the Supreme Court ruled in the cases of *Ballew v. Georgia* (1978) and *Burch and Wrestle v. Louisiana* (1979) that neither a five-member jury operating under a unanimous rule nor a six-member jury operating under a five-of-six rule, were constitutionally permissible. It appears, then, that at least six jurors are required for conviction for criminal trials. The issue of constitutionality of an eight-out-of-twelve rule or a seven-out-of-twelve rule remained unresolved.

Solutions

Practice Problems

1.

	p(conviction) = 0.9		p(conviction) = 0.6		p(conviction) = 0.6	
Size of Jury	Conviction	Acquittal	Conviction	Acquittal	Conviction	Acquittal
10	0.9^{10} $\approx 35\%$	0.1^{10} $\approx 0\%$	0.6^{10} $\approx 0.6\%$	0.4^{10} $\approx 0.01\%$	0.5^{10} $\approx .10\%$	0.5^{10} $\approx .10\%$
6	0.9^{6} $\approx 53\%$	0.1^{6} $\approx 0.0001\%$	0.6^{6} $\approx 4.7\%$	0.4^{6} $\approx .41\%$	0.5^{6} $\approx 1.56\%$	0.5^{6} $\approx 1.56\%$
5	0.9^{5} $\approx 59\%$	0.1^{5} $\approx 0.001\%$	0.6^{5} $\approx 7.8\%$	0.4^{5} $\approx 1.024\%$	0.5^{5} $\approx 3.12\%$	0.5^{5} $\approx 3.12\%$

2. When the likelihood of conviction for each juror is equal to the likelihood of acquittal, the probability of a first-ballot conviction remains equal to the probability of a first-ballot acquittal regardless of the jury size. What is decreasing in each case is the likelihood that *no* verdict will be reached on the first ballot.

Extension Problems

1. 6C5 = 6 different combinations where 5 elements are the same.
   CCCCCA   CCCCAC   CCCACC   CCACCC   CACCCC   ACCCCC
   6C1 = 6 different combinations where 1 element is the same.
   CCCCCA   CCCCAC   CCCACC   CCACCC   CACCCC   ACCCCC
2. a. Unanimous conviction: $0.8^8 = 0.16777 \approx 16.78\%$
   b. Conviction by exactly 7 out of 8: (8C7) $\times$ ($0.8^7 \times 0.2$) = 0.3355 $\approx$ 33.55%
   c. Conviction by at least 7 out of 8: 0.16777 + 0.3355 = 0.50327 $\approx$ 50.33%
   d. Acquittal by at least 7 out of 8: (0.2^8) + (8C7) $\times$ ($0.2^7 \times 0.8$) = 0.000084 $\approx$ 0.008%
3. Answers will vary.

Balancing Equations

Using the Calculator to Solve Equations

Setting the Stage

You will encounter the instruction "Solve for x" quite often in an algebra class, and you have probably already had some experience solving equations algebraically. Being able to use algebra to solve an equation is important, but with a graphing calculator you can also see a visual representation of the solution by graphing the expression on each side as a separate equation. When you do this, the common value of x at the point of intersection of the two lines is the solution of the original equation.

If we keep solving for x, x will never learn how to solve anything for itself!

The Activity

Solve the equation $3x - 5 = {}^-2x + 5$ for x.

If you use conventional algebra, the solution might look like this:

$$3x - 5 = {}^-2x + 5$$
$$\underline{+\,2x \qquad = +2x}$$
$$\underline{5x - 5 = \qquad\quad 5}$$
$$\underline{\qquad\;\; 5 = \qquad + 5}$$
$$5x \;\; = \qquad 10$$
$$\frac{5x}{5} = \frac{10}{5}$$
$$x = 2$$

To solve this equation by graphing, you will graph the expression on each side of the equation as a separate equation. Press $\boxed{\;\text{Y=}\;}$. Enter $3x - 5$ into Y1, and ${}^-2x + 5$ into Y2.

Use the WINDOW settings shown below.

```
WINDOW
 Xmin=-47
 Xmax=47
 Xscl=10
 Ymin=-31
 Ymax=31
 Yscl=10
 Xres=1
```

Press (GRAPH) and you will see the graphs of two lines. The point where the two lines intersect is the solution of the equation. Press (TRACE) and then the right and left arrow keys to travel along the line. If you want to trace on the other line, press the up or down arrow. The 1 or 2 in the upper right corner will tell you which function you are tracing. The two lines intersect when $x = 2$ and $y = 1$. You can confirm this by again pressing the up or down arrow and noticing that the x- and y-values are the same for both functions. The x-value is the solution to the original equation and should confirm the solution that was obtained algebraically.

You can also find the solution using the TABLE function. Press (2nd) [TblSet]. Set TblMin (on the TI-82) or TblStart (on the TI-73 and TI-83) for the starting value for x and ΔTbl for the amount by which you want to change x each time. (In this example, TblMin (TblStart) was set at 0 and ΔTbl at 1.)

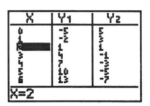

The solution is the x-value for which Y1 = Y2.

Practice Problems

Solve each equation by graphing. Enter the expression on the left side of the equation into Y1 and the expression on the right side into Y2. Sketch the graph.

1. $3x = 21$

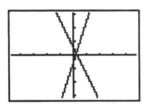

2. $7x = 4x + 21$

3. $3x + 35 = 20$

4. $6x - 4 = 3x + 11$

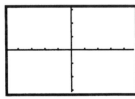

5. $8x + 30.5 = 6.5$

6. $x + 18 = 5$

7. $3x = 4x + 10$

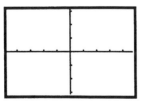

8. $6x - 4 = 26$

9. $15x + 17 = {}^{-}13$

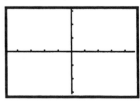

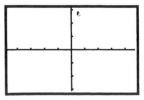

Extension Problems

Most of the time the solution to an equation is not a whole number, and it may be difficult to find the exact value of the solution. There are several ways that you can examine the point of intersection in order to find closer and closer approximations to the solution. One way is to zoom in on the point. Place your cursor near the point of intersection. Press (ZOOM) (2). You can usually find the coordinates of the point to whatever degree of accuracy you require. Another way to zoom in is to use ZOOM Box. Consider this equation: $3x = {}^-2x - 8$. Follow the progression below to see how the graphing calculator can zoom in on the solution.

Standard window

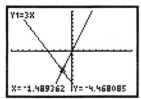

ZOOM Box

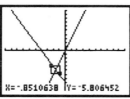

The result

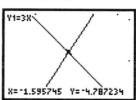

ZOOM Box again

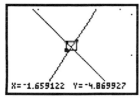

The result

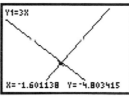

ZOOM Box again

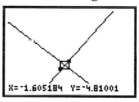

Getting closer

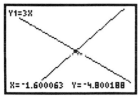

ZOOM once more

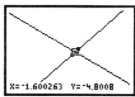

Much closer

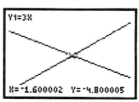

Look at Y2.

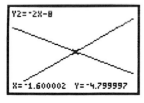

Final ZOOM

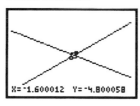

The solution!

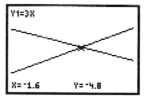

Look at Y2 to confirm.

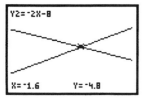

The solution is $x = {}^-1.6$.

If all that zooming makes you dizzy, you can look at the TABLE. Choose a TblMin value that you know is less than the solution (TblStart on the TI-73 and TI-83). Choose an appropriate ΔTbl, and press $\boxed{\text{2nd}}$ [TABLE].

You will notice that the Y1 and Y2 values get closer at first, then farther apart. This means that you will need to study the neighborhood where they are closest, between $x = {}^-2$ and $x = {}^-1$, with a smaller increment for x. Change the TblSet settings as shown.

Again you can see that the solution is $x = {}^-1.6$.

Solve each equation by zooming and by looking at a table of values. Find each solution accurate to three decimal places.

1. $2x + 7 = {}^-6x + 5$
2. $7x - 3 = 2x + 1$
3. $4x - 7 = {}^-3x + 9$
4. $x^2 - 3 = 2x + 1$

More Than Graphs, Revised Edition • ©2004 Key Curriculum Press

Balancing Equations

Objective: To visualize the solution to a single-variable linear equation
Materials needed: TI-73, TI-82, TI-83, or TI-83 Plus graphing calculator
Appropriate level: Algebra and pre-algebra
Time involved: One and one-half hours, or two class periods
Preparation: Understanding of how to solve single-variable linear equations

The ability to solve, or balance, an equation is one of the fundamental skills learned by first-year algebra students. All too often, the students learn this process by learning a set of rules, which they apply by guessing which one to use. (Divide? No, that's not it. Subtract. OK. That works.) The only checking they do is to select another operation when their answer doesn't turn out to be a whole number.

This lesson doesn't forgo any of the traditional building blocks necessary to learn this process;

it just enhances them by giving a visual confirmation of the solution. Finding an exact solution by graphing alone can be very challenging, and sometimes impossible, particularly when complex fractions or irrational numbers are part of the solution. As a teacher you will need to decide whether you want your students to also solve each equation algebraically. The graph can be used to check whether the algebraic solution is reasonable.

Solutions

Practice Problems

1. $x = 7$
2. $x = 7$
3. $x = {}^-5$
4. $x = 5$
5. $x = {}^-3$
6. $x = {}^-26$
7. $x = {}^-10$
8. $x = 5$
9. $x = {}^-2$

Extension Problems

1. $x = {}^-0.25$
2. $x = 0.8$
3. $x = 2.286$
4. $x = {}^-1.236$ and $x = 3.236$

Functional Flooring

Using Graphs to Find Solutions

Setting the Stage

You just started working at your new job at the local Fantastic Floors store. Annie Aerobic has come to you for help in choosing materials for a new floor for her exercise room. Unfortunately, she forgot to bring the dimensions with her. However, she remembers that the space she needs to cover is a rectangle with an area of 42 feet square and a perimeter of 29 feet. Annie is disappointed to have forgotten the measurements, but you assure her that it will be a piece of cake to figure out the possible lengths and widths of the floor using a combination of graphs and tables on your always-handy graphing calculator.

The Activity

Analyzing the Problem

The first step is to model the situation using equations. If you let x represent the width and y represent the length of the floor space, you can express the area relationship using the equation $xy = 42$ or $y = 42/x$. Enter this equation as Y1. The perimeter relationship can be described with the equation $2x + 2y = 29$. This is the same as $x + y = 14.5$, or $y = 14.5 - x$. Enter this equation as Y2.

The next step is to graph the equations using a friendly window. Use these WINDOW settings:

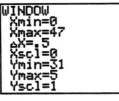

TI-73

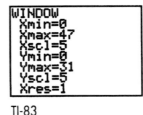

TI-83

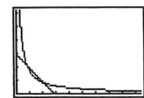

Press GRAPH. There appear to be two intersection points. What are they? These two points are solutions to the simultaneous equations.

Confirming the Solution

Press TRACE and use the right and left arrows to position the cursor over the location where the functions appear to cross. Press the up and down arrows to move from Y1 to Y2. If there is no change when you press the up and down arrows, then the point is indeed a common solution to the two equations.

What advice would you give Annie? Are there really two possibilities?

Practice Problems

Graph each pair of functions and find the common solution(s).

1. $y = {}^{-}x^2 + 2$
   $y = x - 4$

2. $y = x^2$
   $y = x + 6$

3. $y = \frac{12}{x}$
   $y^2 = 25 - x^2$
   (Note: This second equation represents a circle. Because the equation of a circle is not a function, you will have to enter two equations: $y = \sqrt{25 - x^2}$ and $y = {}^{-}\sqrt{25 - x^2}$. When tracing to find the points of intersection, you will have to arrow up and down to move among the three functions.)

4. $y = x^2 - 4x + 3$
   $y = x^3 - 6x^2 + 11x + 3$

Extension Problems

Meanwhile, back at the ranch . . .

1. You have decided to fence in an area for your new lambs along one side of your barn. You have 64 m of fencing material available and would like the total area to be 480 m². Write two equations that describe this situation and graph them on your calculator to find the dimensions of the pen.

2. You read in the latest *Goat Fancy Magazine* that the average goat needs to have about 60 ft² in which to graze. You want to tie up your goat along a fence so that it will have a semicircular grazing area. How long should the rope be so that your goat will have 60 ft² of grazing area?

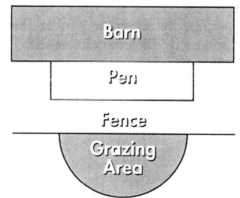

Functional Flooring

Objective:	To graphically find the solutions of a pair of simultaneous equations
Materials needed:	TI-73, TI-82, TI-83, or TI-83 Plus graphing calculator
Appropriate level:	Algebra and pre-algebra
Time involved:	One hour or class period
Preparation:	Familiarity with Cartesian coordinates

This lesson covers many of the same topics as the *Common Solutions* activity.

Students find the intersections of a pair of simultaneous equations by using the TRACE feature and adjusting the WINDOW settings to get a clearer look. You may want to remind your students how to create friendly WINDOWs. The range of the x- and y-settings must be factors respectively of the number of horizontal and vertical pixels on the screen. For more information on friendly windows, see the *Circles and Eggs* activity.

Discuss situations with your students in which simultaneous functions have two solutions. How do the two solutions impact the problem modeled by the functions? In the example in the activity, the two solutions are (4, 10.5) and (10.5, 4), but these solutions actually provide the same information. In Extension Problem 1, however, there are two ways to design the pen that satisfy the requirements.

You may want to introduce students to the table function. To use the table function, press 2nd [TblSet], set TblStart (TblMin on the TI-82) for an x-value just below the suspected intersection, and choose a value for ΔTbl. By changing the ΔTbl, you can examine smaller and smaller x-intervals in the table. If the listed values for Y1 and Y2 are equal, then you have found a common solution of both functions.

You may want to introduce students to the CALC intersect function on the TI-82 and TI-83. To find the intersection of two functions entered in the calculator, press 2nd [CALC] and choose 5 (intersect). Position the cursor on the first function and press ENTER. Then use the up or down arrow to move the cursor to the second function and press ENTER again. Lastly, position the cursor on or near the point of intersection and press ENTER again. The calculator will respond with the coordinates of the point of intersection.

Solutions

Practice Problems

1. $(2, -2)$, $(-3, -7)$
2. $(-2, 4)$, $(3, 90)$
3. $(3, 4)$, $(-3, -4)$
4. $(0, 3)$

Extension Problems

1. $2x + y = 64$, and $xy = 480$
   The pen can be 12 m by 40 m or 20 m by 24 m.
2. $y = 0.5\pi x^2$ and $y = 60$
   The rope should be about 6.18 ft long.

Survivor—An Elimination Game FUNC
Using Your Equation-Writing Skills

Setting the Stage

In this game, you and your opponent will each have a team of seven points, which you'll graph on a calculator screen. The object of the game is to write equations that pass through as many of your opponent's team members or points as possible, and to place your team members so that it is not easy for your opponent to write equations that will pass through them.

The Activity

Rules

Each player places seven points on the screen. The players then alternate turns trying to obliterate each other's points by graphing equations that pass through the opponent's points. A round consists of two alternating turns for each player. At the end of a round, each person's score is the number of his or her points that have survived. To start the next round, each player plots seven new points. The game continues for five rounds. The player with the highest score wins.

Playing the Game

First, build the playing field by pressing (ZOOM) (6) to define a 20 × 20 playing area between +10 and −10 on both axes.

Player 1 loads the coordinates (x, y) for seven points of his or her choice into L1 and L2. Player 2 then loads seven points into L3 and L4 and presses (2nd) [QUIT]. All points must be visible within the defined area of the playing field. Be sure to turn the grid on ((2nd) [FORMAT] on the TI-73 and TI-83, and (WINDOW) FORMAT on the TI-82).

Player 1 plots his or her team of points on the grid using the scatter plot in Stat Plot1 with L1 and L2 selected. Player 1 marks his or her team members with a ◻. Player 2 puts his or her team on the field using the scatter plot in Stat Plot2 with L3, L4, and the + mark selected. Press (GRAPH) to display the points.

Player 1 starts by entering an equation into Y= that he or she thinks will run over as many of the other team's points as possible. After Player 1 has entered and graphed an equation, it's Player 2's turn. Each player gets two turns in a round.

Use the TRACE key to settle arguments. Points closer than 0.1 to lines or curves are scored as hits. Players are not forgiven for running over their own team members.

Functions need not be restricted to linear equations.

More Than Graphs, Revised Edition • ©2004 Key Curriculum Press

Survivor—An Elimination Game

Objective:	To develop skills in writing equations
Materials needed:	TI-73, TI-82, TI-83, or TI-83 Plus graphing calculator
Appropriate level:	Algebra and pre-algebra
Time involved:	One hour or class period
Preparation:	Experience with writing equations to fit a set of points

While playing the game, my students quickly learned that it is disadvantageous to choose a set of collinear points, so they adopted strategies of placing them at random intervals all around the screen. They discovered, in short order, that having the calculator compute a line of best fit has no advantage, since the regression line may not actually "roll over" any of the data points.

If students are allowed to use a second calculator, they have the option of experimenting with built-in regressions. The most successful players were the ones that opted to select three points, input them in L1 and L2, and have the calculator compute a quadratic or cubic regression to fit the three points. You should decide with your students what the rules are for using the calculator and whether a player may use a second calculator to calculate regression equations. You may want to wait until students come up with this idea. The game will become more sophisticated as students' mathematical skills improve. Therefore, this game can be played throughout the year and will continue to challenge the students. Some students even take the game home to play against their parents.

Booleans

Solving Inequations Using Boolean Algebra

Setting the Stage

George Boole was a nineteenth-century mathematician who contributed to the development of a branch of algebra in which all math statements are evaluated as being true or false. Those that are true are assigned the value 1, and those that are false are designated by 0. This algebra is called *Boolean algebra,* and it has had an amazing impact on all of our lives

with the development of the computer. All computers—even your graphing calculator—rely on this type of algebra because the values 1 for true and 0 for false are very well suited to the binary systems used by computers. In this activity, you will use Boolean algebra to solve inequations with your calculator.

The Activity

The calculator uses the ideas of Boolean algebra to plot 0 and 1 as *y*-values to tell you whether an algebraic statement is true or false. When setting up your window, you can choose values for Ymax and Ymin that are rather close together because the only possible *y*-values are 0 or 1. For this activity, use the following WINDOW settings:

```
WINDOW
 Xmin=-47
 Xmax=47
 Xscl=10
 Ymin=-3.1
 Ymax=3.1
 Yscl=1
 Xres=1
```

Change the MODE setting to Dot. Activate AxesOff in the FORMAT menu.

Consider the inequation $2x + 6 \geq 12$.

The conventional algebra solution might look something like this:

$$2x + 6 \geq 12$$
$$\underline{ -6 \quad -6}$$
$$2x \quad \geq \quad 6$$
$$\frac{2x}{2} \geq \frac{6}{2}$$
$$x \geq 3$$

More Than Graphs, Revised Edition • ©2004 Key Curriculum Press

Therefore, the inequation $2x + 6 \geq 12$ is true whenever $x \geq 3$.

How can you see the solution to this inequation using your calculator?

Press $\boxed{\text{Y=}}$ and enter Y1 = $2x + 6 \geq 12$. The inequalities are listed under $\boxed{\text{2nd}}$ [TEST] ($\boxed{\text{2nd}}$ [TEXT] on the TI-73). Press $\boxed{\text{GRAPH}}$. The graph should confirm the algebraic solution. Press $\boxed{\text{TRACE}}$ to explore the x-values along the line.

False (0) at x = 2   True (1) at x = 3

You can see that the y-value changed from false (0) to true (1) when the x-value reached 3. (If no break is visible, you can enlarge the window by multiplying Xmin and Xmax by factors of 10, 100, or 1000.)

By changing the viewing window, you can study the function closer to where it makes the jump between false and true. Try this:

In the WINDOW screen, Set Xmin at the *lower bound* of the break (Xmin = 2).

On the Home screen, store a value of 0.02 for ΔX. To do this, press .02 $\boxed{\text{STO►}}$ $\boxed{\text{VARS}}$ $\boxed{1}$ ($\boxed{\text{2nd}}$ [VARS] on the TI-73); scroll down until you find ΔX and then press $\boxed{\text{ENTER}}$. (ΔX is the eighth choice on the TI-83 and TI-73 and the seventh choice on the TI-82.)

Now look at your WINDOW screen and see what happened to Xmax. The new Xmax value should be 3.88. The value of ΔX determines the width of each pixel, which determines how much the x-value will change each time you press a right or left arrow key when tracing. Xmax will automatically change to the value that it needs to be in order for this to happen.

Press $\boxed{\text{GRAPH}}$.

Your new graph screen should look like the one at the right. Notice that when you trace on this graph, the increment for x is 0.02.

The process can be repeated again using 2.98 as the new Xmin and 0.002 as the new ΔX. (By pressing $\boxed{\text{2nd}}$ [ENTRY] on the Home screen, you can use $\boxed{\text{2nd}}$ [INS] and $\boxed{\text{DEL}}$ to edit the previous STO command.) If you do this, you'll see that the break from false to true still comes just below 3, but even closer to 3. Are you convinced that the solution for this problem is $x \geq 3$?

Practice Problems

Solve each inequation. Sketch a graph and label the *x*-values on either side of the break. Name three *x*-values that would make the inequation true.

1. $x + 7 > 9$

2. $3x < 15$

3. $|x| < x$

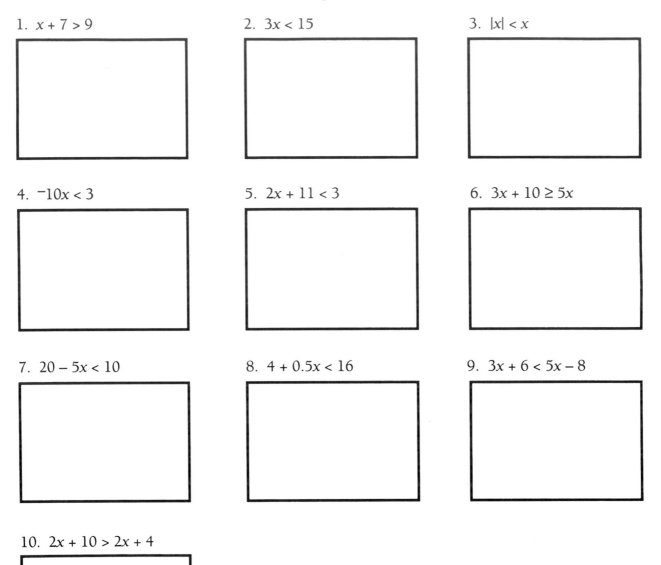

4. $^-10x < 3$

5. $2x + 11 < 3$

6. $3x + 10 \geq 5x$

7. $20 - 5x < 10$

8. $4 + 0.5x < 16$

9. $3x + 6 < 5x - 8$

10. $2x + 10 > 2x + 4$

Extension Problems

You can also solve an inequation using a strategy similar to what you used in the *Balancing Equations* activity. Try this with the sample problem $2x + 6 \geq 12$. Graph each side of the inequation as a separate equation. Enter Y1 = $2x + 6$ and Y2 = 12.

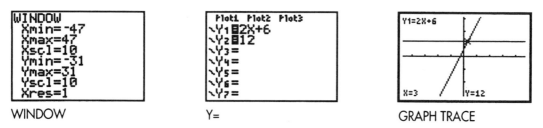

WINDOW   Y=   GRAPH TRACE

These two equations have the same value at $x = 3$. This graph shows that Y1 = $2x + 6$ is greater than Y2 = 12 to the right of the point where $x = 3$. Y2 is greater than Y1 to the left of $x = 3$. The question is: When is $2x + 6 \geq 12$? This occurs at and to the right of $x = 3$, so the solution is $x \geq 3$.

1. Use this method to verify your solutions to the Practice Problems.
2. Describe what you think would happen using this method if you tried to solve an inequation that was always true.
3. Describe what you think would happen using this method if you tried to solve an inequation that was always false.

Booleans

Objective:	To solve inequations by graphing
Materials needed:	TI-73, TI-82, TI-83, or TI-83 Plus graphing calculator
Appropriate level:	Algebra and pre-algebra
Time involved:	One hour or class period
Preparation:	Experience with number lines

In this lesson, I tried to give students a graphic representation of inequations. The ΔX function is a much faster and precise way of zooming in to microscopic levels to study this than changing the WINDOW settings. Just remember that ΔX is added to whatever the current Xmin is until the Xmax value is at its limit according to the number of pixels available. Xmax is a dependent value that is defined after ΔX is stored.

You could also explore these inequations using the TABLE function. However, changing the ΔX increment will not automatically change the ΔTbl value.

There is an entire branch of mathematics known as *Boolean algebra* that is seldom explored at the middle-school level, but this activity is entirely within the reach of these students and offers an excellent lead-in to logic problems. Boolean algebra is one of the underlying themes in understanding the digital circuitry of electronics because in digital circuitry each data bit must correspond to a 0 (off) or a 1 (on).

Solutions

Practice Problems

Each problem is true (or has a value of 1) for these cases.

1. $x > 2$
2. $x < 5$
3. Not true for any value of x
4. $x \geq {}^{-}3$
5. $x < {}^{-}4$
6. $x < 5$
7. $x > 2$
8. $x < 24$
9. $x > 7$
10. Always true for any value of x

Extension Problems

1. Answers will vary.
2. If the inequation is always true, the two lines will be coincident.
3. If the inequation is always false, the two lines will not intersect.

Snafooz!

Collecting and Analyzing Experimental Data

Setting the Stage

Collecting and organizing experimental data is an
important component of the scientific method. In
this experiment, you and your classmates will
collect data by timing yourselves while you put
together *Snafooz* puzzles. Afterwards, you can use
the calculator to analyze the data and try to figure
out which of the puzzles is the most difficult.

The Activity

Collecting the Data

Snafooz cubes come in six colors. Be sure that you have all six puzzle pieces before beginning. The
object of the puzzle is to fit the pieces together to form a cube. Each person in the group should
take turns solving each of the puzzles, recording the color of the puzzle and the time (in seconds)
required to complete the puzzle. If you can't complete the puzzle within 10 minutes, then record
the puzzle time as incomplete.

Entering the Data

Collect the data from the class. Let each list represent a different color. Enter the time in
seconds needed to solve each puzzle for each class member. Assign the lists as follows:

L1—Red   L4—Green
L2—Blue   L5—Orange
L3—Yellow   L6—Purple

It is not necessary for each list to have the same number of entries, so it is all right if some
members of your team do not solve all of the puzzles in the allotted time period.

Analyzing the Data

Use the STAT PLOT function to construct a histogram for each data set.

Press ⬚ 2nd ⬚ [STAT PLOT] ⬚ 1 ⬚ (⬚ 2nd ⬚ [PLOT] ⬚ 1 ⬚ on the TI-73) and turn Plot1 On. Choose
Histogram. Set the L-value for the list to be studied and set the Frequency at 1.

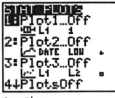

Stat Plotter

TI-73

TI-82

TI-83

Press [GRAPH] to see a histogram. Remember you'll have to set your window using appropriate values.

Press [STAT] CALC [1] ([2nd] [STAT] CALC [1] on the TI-73) to see the 1–Var Stats.

TI-73 Screens

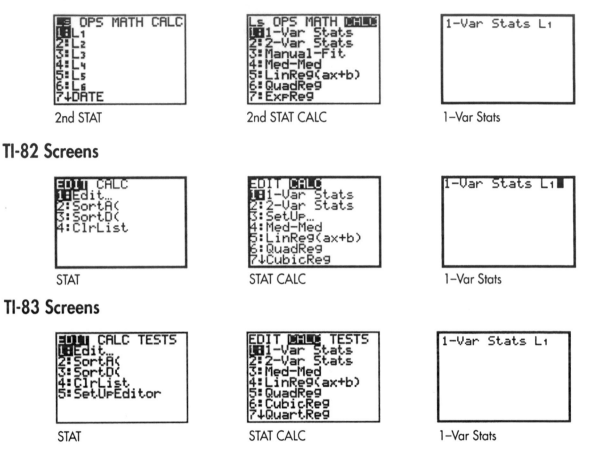

2nd STAT 2nd STAT CALC 1–Var Stats

TI-82 Screens

STAT STAT CALC 1–Var Stats

TI-83 Screens

STAT STAT CALC 1–Var Stats

Practice Problems

1. Make a histogram of the solving times for each puzzle color. Sketch each histogram on your paper and label it by color.
2. Press [STAT] CALC [1] ([2nd] [STAT] CALC [1] on the TI-73) to compute single-variable statistics for each column. You will have to tell the calculator the appropriate list name each time.
3. Make a table displaying the average, minimum, and maximum time for each puzzle color.
4. Using the information from Problems 1 and 3, rank the puzzles in order of difficulty.
5. How does this ranking compare with your own impression of the difficulty of the puzzles?
6. Collect the data from each member of the class, and make a class histogram for each color. Describe how class results compare to your individual results.

7. Now, try something different. Solve the same puzzle several times in a row, recording the time it takes you to solve it each time. Graph a histogram of these values.
8. What does it mean if each bar is shorter than the one before it?
9. Make a scatter plot of this data, and find a regression equation that seems to fit the data. Write several sentences explaining what this equation and its graph tell you about your learning rate.
10. Compare your learning-rate equation and graph with those of other team members. Are they all similar or different? Write a sentence or two explaining what you think this means.

Extension Problem

Try this activity with another kind of puzzle, perhaps some wire topological puzzles. Do an analysis to see which of the puzzles is most difficult. Also do an analysis to determine what the learning rate might be.

Snafooz!

Objective:	To collect and analyze data from an experiment
Materials needed:	TI-73, TI-82, TI-83, or TI-83 Plus graphing calculator, Snafooz cubes, graphing paper, stopwatch or watch with a second hand
Appropriate level:	Algebra and pre-algebra
Time involved:	One hour or class period
Preparation:	Introduction to the statistical functions on the TI-73, TI-82, TI-83, or TI-83 Plus graphing calculators

I originally saw this activity done by Steve Ackley, Jan Palowski, Ron Kady, Ron Gonzales, Barb Branch, Rich Horner, Murney Bell, and Miguel Medina at the Woodrow Wilson Institute at Princeton.

Although it's a bit of a hassle to set up, *Snafooz* had one of the highest ratings by students of any of the graphing calculator lessons. Students enjoy solving the puzzles and analyzing what the data means. There are no penalties for students who take longer, and each student seemed to feel a sense of accomplishment when a puzzle was completed, no matter how long it took. The fastest that any student was able to complete a Snafooz cube was 11 seconds. We had considerable discussion about whether this was simply luck or reflected actual skill. Nonetheless, that completion time was a source of great pride for that student.

An interesting extension of this activity is to exchange unmarked class data histograms between classes that have done the same experiment and ask the students to determine which graphs from the other class correspond to which color and difficulty level. Most students will have a puzzle or two from the selection that they consider to be particularly challenging from their personal experience. Rather than ask the students to study the statistical similarities and measures of central tendencies of the two classes, I allowed them to make their judgments based on their own individual experiences. This led to an interesting writing assignment on bias or prejudice.

Solutions

Practice Problems

Answers will vary.

Extension Problem

Answers will vary.

Problems of Interest I

Using Recursive Routines to Calculate Interest and Loan Balances

Setting the Stage

If everyone went to a bank at the same time to withdraw their money, you can probably imagine that the bank would not be happy. Banks invest the money of their depositors, so they don't have all that money on hand. They charge interest to those who borrow money from them, and they pay a lesser amount of interest to the depositors who let their money be used. The difference between these two rates is what allows banks and other lending institutions to stay in business. The amount of cash a bank has on hand is usually only a very small fraction of its total assets.

When interest is calculated, the calculation is at a fraction of the yearly rate. An interest rate of 12% yearly might be compounded at a rate of 6% semiannually, or 3% quarterly, or 1% monthly. How often a bank compounds interest will make a difference in interest you earn or pay in one year.

Interest compounded *annually* on $20,000 at a rate of 12% would give you a balance of

$$20,000 + 20,000 \cdot 0.12 = \$22,400$$

Interest compounded *semiannually* on $20,000 at an annual rate of 12% would give you a balance of

$20,000 + 20,000 \cdot 0.12 \cdot (6/12) = \$21,200$	Balance after first 6 months
$21,200 + 21,200 \cdot 0.12 \cdot (6/12) = \$22,472$	Balance after 1 year

Interest compounded *quarterly* on $20,000 at an annual rate of 12% would give you a balance of

$20,000 + 20,000 \cdot 0.12 \cdot (3/12) = \$20,600.00$	Balance after first 3 months
$20,600 + 20,600 \cdot 0.12 \cdot (3/12) = \$21,218.00$	Balance after second 3 months
$21,218 + 21,218 \cdot 0.12 \cdot (3/12) = \$21,854.54$	Balance after third 3 months
$21,854.54 + 21,854.54 \cdot 0.12 \cdot (3/12) = \$22,510.18$	Balance after 1 year

The Activity

Before starting this activity, you may want to set the decimal point to fixed rather than floating. The problems in this activity deal with money, so you'll need only two places after the decimal point. You can do this by pressing [MODE] and selecting 2 in the Float line.

TI-73

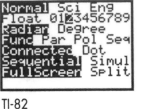

TI-82

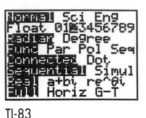

TI-83

From the above examples, you can determine the formula for calculating the balance.

Next balance = Previous balance + Previous balance · Interest rate · Time period

Notice that the time period is how often the interest is compounded in terms of an annual rate. So, for an annual rate compounded every 6 months, use 6/12.

You can do this calculation very easily on your calculator using what is called a *recursive routine*. You are calculating recursively whenever you use the last answer to compute the next answer. Do this next problem to see how it works.

You deposit $1000 in a bank that pays 5% interest per year compounded annually. How much is in your account after 4 years?

Press 1000 [ENTER]. This is called *seeding the calculator* by telling it what the first term in the sequence is. Then press [2nd] [ANS]. ANS represents the previous balance. Now enter the rest of the formula. You should see the expression below on your calculator screen.

$$ANS + ANS \cdot .05 \cdot 1$$

The balance after each time period, a year in this case, will be displayed each time you press [ENTER].

You can see that after 4 years there will be $1215.51 in this account.

If you were to take your money to a different bank that paid 5% interest, but compounded the interest quarterly, you would enter the expression below.

$$ANS + ANS \cdot .05 \cdot (3/12)$$

You would need to look at the value of the account over 16 time periods to cover a 4-year period, because each time period is only 3 months, or 3/12.

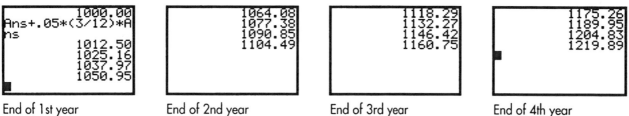

| End of 1st year | End of 2nd year | End of 3rd year | End of 4th year |

The balance at this bank after 4 years is $1219.89.

Amortization is the process of paying off a loan over a period of time. It is very similar to interest on a deposit except that your payment is subtracted from the principal, and then the interest is recalculated.

This is the formula for amortization:

Balance = Previous balance + Previous balance · Interest · Time period − Payment

For a loan payment of $50/month, and an interest rate of 5%, the expression you would enter in the calculator after entering the seed value is shown below.

$$\text{ANS} + \text{ANS} \cdot .05 \cdot 1/12 - 50$$

At 15% interest (a typical rate for credit cards), how long will it take a borrower to pay back $1000 if the payments are $50/month and no more purchases are made?

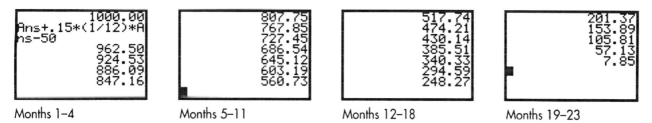

| Months 1–4 | Months 5–11 | Months 12–18 | Months 19–23 |

Paying off the loan at $50/month would take 23 months. The last payment would be $7.85.

Notice that the first $50 payment reduced the principal by only $37.50. The last payment reduced the principal by $49.78.

Practice Problems

1. You have $5000 to invest for your college education. Find the value of your account at each of these banks after 5 years.
    a. Happy Savings and Loan pays 4%, compounded annually.
    b. Taxpayer's Credit Union pays 3.5%, compounded monthly.
    c. Friendly Mutual offers new depositors a $20 one-time bonus and pays 3.75%, compounded quarterly.
    d. Greater Northwest National Bank pays 3.9%, compounded semiannually.

2. The NorthAmericard Credit Company charges an 18% interest rate on outstanding balances. VISTA charges 12%, but has a $50 yearly membership fee. Which company offers the best deal for a customer who owes $800 and makes payments of $50/month?

3. You have been yearning for a new stereo system with the works and have found it for $2300 at a discount electronics store. You have a credit card that charges 16% interest on outstanding balances. You figure that you can make payments of $150/month.
   a. How long will it take you to pay off the stereo if you make no other purchases on your credit card?
   b. When you have paid off the stereo, how much interest will you have paid?
   c. If you decided to save the $150 each month in a long-term account that pays 8.5% interest, how long would it take you to save up for the stereo?
   d. How much interest would you have earned in that time?

Extension Problem

Look through newspapers and mail that may arrive at your house. What other incentives do different banks offer to entice borrowers and depositors to do business with them, besides altering the interest rate and membership fees? From a customer's point of view, do these incentives justify changing banks? What risks may be involved? You may want to discuss this problem with your parents and find out their opinions. Do a mathematical analysis using what you have learned in this activity. Write several paragraphs justifying your answer.

More Than Graphs, Revised Edition • ©2004 Key Curriculum Press

TEACHER NOTES

Problems of Interest I

Objective: To learn about recursive routines and use them to calculate interest and loan balances
Materials needed: TI-73, TI-82, TI-83, or TI-83 Plus graphing calculator
Appropriate level: Algebra and pre-algebra
Time involved: One hour or class period
Preparation: Familiarity with abbreviations and vocabulary used in banking

I wanted to write a lesson that students might share with their parents. In most families, someone has a credit card and students may even have their own bank accounts. Informed consumers need to understand how differing factors can affect how much interest they earn and pay. These are things that parents can offer insights into, and I believe those insights can reinforce this type of lesson. You might want to encourage students to share this activity with their parents, and have a discussion about how interest rates affect their lives.

In this activity students use a recursive routine entered directly on the Home screen. The next activity covers the same concepts, but introduces students to the Sequence Mode, which is a built-in feature on the TI-82 and TI-83 calculators; it is not available on the TI-73.

Solutions

Practice Problems

1. After 5 years
   a. Happy Savings and Loan balance is $6083.26.
   b. Taxpayer's Credit Union balance is $5954.71.
   c. Friendly Mutual balance is $6049.99.
   d. Greater Northwest National Bank balance is $6065.16.
2. NorthAmericard—Total payments = $871.40
          VISTA—Total payments = $885.99
3. a. It will take 18 months to pay off the balance, with a last payment of $39.82.
   b. You will have paid $289.82 in interest.
   c. It will take 15 months to save up the $2300, with a last deposit of $100.52.
   d. You will have earned $100.52 in interest.

Extension Problem

Answers will vary.

Problems of Interest II
Using the Sequence Mode on the TI-82 and TI-83

Setting the Stage

With larger loans over long time periods, it is not uncommon for you to pay more in interest than the amount you actually borrowed. The time period as well as the amount that you pay each month significantly affects the total cost of the loan. In this activity you will learn about the Seq mode on your calculator. This mode allows you to build a table of values and graph the results so that you can more closely examine what happens when you invest or borrow money. In the Seq mode you can even compare two different interest rates at the same time.

The Activity

You can use the calculator to build a compound interest table. First you will need to change to Seq mode. Press $\boxed{\text{MODE}}$ and select Seq. You can also select a fixed decimal point of two places rather than a floating decimal since most of the problems deal with monetary amounts.

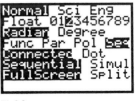

TI-82

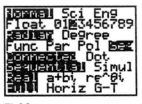

TI-83

Working in Seq mode is tricky and may seem very confusing at first. Be sure to have your calculator in hand and do each step as it is presented.

You deposit $1000 in a bank that pays 5% interest compounded annually. How much is in the account after 10 years?

The equation you would use to calculate this is

Present balance = Previous balance + Previous balance · 0.05 · Time period

Press $\boxed{\text{Y=}}$ and you will see three sequence functions (two sequence functions on the TI-82): U_n, V_n, and W_n (read U sub n, V sub n, and W sub n). This means you can enter up to three sequences. For this problem, however, you will use only the first one, U_n. The variable n

More Than Graphs, Revised Edition • ©2004 Key Curriculum Press

represents the number of years, and Un represents the present balance. The previous balance will be represented by U$n-1$. So the expression you want to enter for Un is U$n-1$ + U$n-1 \cdot .05 \cdot 1$.

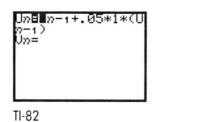

TI-82

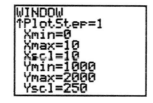

TI-83

Setting Windows on the TI-83

The U key is created by pressing [2nd] [7]. The n key is made by using the key normally used for X in the function mode [X,T,Θ,n].

U (nMin) is the beginning value of $1000.

Now you need to set the WINDOW values. The window for this problem will look like this:

These WINDOW values affect the sequence calculation:

nMin   start at 0 years
nMax   end at 10 years

These WINDOW values set the graphing window:

Xmin   usually the same as nMin
Xmax   usually the same as nMax
Ymin   the minimum balance ($1000 in this case)
Ymax   more than the maximum balance

Setting Windows on the TI-82

Now you need to set the WINDOW values. The window for this problem will look like this:

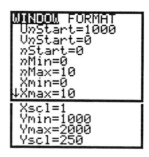

These WINDOW values affect the sequence calculation:

UnStart   the original investment
nStart   start at 0 years
nMin   0
nMax   end at 10 years

These WINDOW values set the graphing window:

Xmin   usually the same as nMin
Xmax   usually the same as nMax
Ymin   the minimum balance
Ymax   more than the maximum balance

Tables and Graphs on the TI-82 and TI-83

Press [2nd] [TblSet] and set TblStart = 0 (Tbl min = 0 on the TI-82) and ΔTbl = 1.

Press [2nd] [TABLE] to
see the table of yearly
balances.

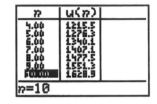

Press [GRAPH] to see a
graph of the balances.

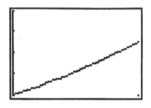

If instead you wanted to look at the balances for interest compounded semiannually, the WINDOW settings would all be the same except nMax, Xmax, and Un. Set nMax and Xmax to 20 because there will now be 20 pay periods.

You will have to slightly modify the equation for Un because the interest will be recalculated every 1/2 year.

$$U_n = U_{n-1} + U_{n-1} \cdot .05 \cdot 6/12$$

Now look at the new table and graph:

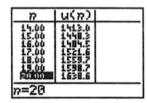   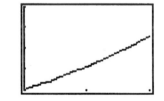

What changes would you have to make for compounding quarterly and compounding monthly?

You can also create an amortization table. At 15% interest (very close to the current rate for credit cards), how long will it take you to pay back a $1000 loan if the payments are $50/month?

Set up the problem by changing nMax and Xmax to 25, and change the formula for Un.

$$U_n = U_{n-1} + U_{n-1} \cdot .15 \cdot 1/12 - 50$$

Look at the table and you can see that after 23 months, you will owe $7.85, so it will take 24 months to pay off the loan. This means that the total amount of all payments will be $1157.85, so you will have paid $157.85 in interest.

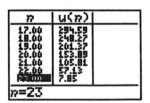

Practice Problems

1. On her twentieth birthday, Geraldine's grandparents invest $7500 in a savings account to start her retirement fund. The interest rate is 8% compounded annually.
   a. If Geraldine plans to retire when she is 50, how much will be in the account?
   b. How much would be in the account if she added $2000 to it each year?
   c. Geraldine decides she would like to have $1,000,000 in the account when she retires at age 50. If she were to add the same amount each year, how much would that amount have to be?
2. Dream about buying a new car. Suppose you can make a $1000 down payment and want to pay off the loan in 48 months. Select your dream car from the classified ads, include a written description, and calculate the monthly payment necessary to completely pay it off with the 48th payment using guess-and-check on your calculator. How much total interest would you pay?
3. What payment would pay off your dream car in 60 months? How much total interest would you pay?
4. If you wanted to purchase a home valued at $100,000 but had only $10,000 for a down payment, you would have to finance the remainder of the purchase price. Home mortgages are usually for 15 or 30 years. Figure out the monthly payment you would need to pay off the house in 30 years at 8% interest. Mortgage rates are usually lower if you finance a loan for a shorter period of time. What payment amount would you need to pay off the same loan at 7.75% over a 15-year period? Compare the total amount you would have to pay for each loan.

Extension Problems

Applying These Principles to Planet Earth

1. The methods you've learned for calculating interest can also be used for other growth situations. Below are listed a number of the world's countries, their populations, and rates of growth. Complete the table to forecast their populations for the years 2008 and 2018.

Country	1998 Population	Growth Rate	Projected Population in 2008	Projected Population in 2018
Australia	18,613,087	+0.7%		
Canada	30,675,398	+0.5%		
China	1,236,914,658	+0.9%		
Congo	49,000,511	+3.2%		
Germany	82,079,454	−0.2%		
India	984,003,683	+1.7%		
Mexico	98,552,776	+2.1%		
Singapore	3,490,356	+0.9%		
USA	270,311,758	+0.6%		

Data excerpted from the *1999 World Almanac*

2. The population of Mexico is growing at a faster rate than that of the United States. When will their populations be the same based on this model? What factors might affect the accuracy of this prediction? (Hint: You can use both sequence equations (U_n and V_n) for this problem and look at either the table or the graph to find the year in which the populations are the same.)

Problems of Interest II

Objective: To use the calculator to build a table of loan installments
Materials needed: TI-82, TI-83, or TI-83 Plus graphing calculator
Appropriate level: Algebra
Time involved: One hour or class period
Preparation: Experience with calculating balances recursively

Using the Sequence mode can be very challenging for some students. Besides the strange-looking formulas, there are a lot of WINDOW settings, and these can be quite confusing. It is highly recommended that students do the *Problems of Interest I* activity first. Try to help them make the connection between ANS and U_{n-1} (written as $u(n-1)$ on the TI-83).

The tables can help students see changes over time for loan and investment balances. It's actually possible to have two or three calculations occur at the same time, possibly with different interest rates or down payments,

and have one displayed as a U_n-value and the other(s) as V_n-values and W_n-values. They will be displayed in the same table. Graphing in Seq mode lets students visualize what is happening when interest is compounded as well as seeing how loan balances decrease over time.

The Extension Problems show students how they can apply this method to a population growth problem, which can lead to some interesting class discussions. Students can also see how methods they learn in math class can be applied to other subject areas as well.

Solutions

Practice Problems

1. a. After 30 years, she would have $100,627 in the account.
    b. $327,193
    c. Approximately $8000
2. Answers will vary.
3. Answers will vary.
4. The 30-year loan at 8% would have a monthly payment of $660.50 and a last monthly payment of $493.80. The total paid for this loan would be $237,613.30. The 15-year loan at 7.5% would have a monthly payment of $926.50 and a last payment of $878.72. The total paid for this loan would be $138,927.22.

Extension Problems

1. Population predictions

Country	1998 Population	Growth Rate	Projected Population in 2008	Projected Population in 2018
Australia	18,613,087	+0.7%	19,957,821	21,399,706
Canada	30,675,398	+0.5%	32,244,142	33,893,112
China	1,236,914,658	+0.9%	1,352,855,459	1,479,663,841
Congo	49,000,511	+3.2%	67,142,512	92,001,425
Germany	82,079,454	⁻0.2%	80,452,561	78,857,914
India	984,003,683	+1.7%	1,164,679,022	1,378,528,605
Mexico	98,552,776	+2.1%	121,318,291	149,342,599
Singapore	3,490,356	+0.9%	3,817,521	4,175,352
USA	270,311,758	+0.6%	286,975,449	304,666,393

2. According to this model, the population of Mexico will overtake that of the United States in 70 years or in the year 2067. Answers will vary.

Common Solutions

Using the CALC Feature to Explore Functions

Setting the Stage

Fiona, the frugal carpenter, builds stools and chairs. All the stools have three legs, and all the chairs have four legs. Fiona wishes to build 28 pieces of furniture and has 100 furniture legs. How many stools and chairs can Fiona build without wasting any legs?

The Activity

There are two situations in this problem, and they can be defined with two equations:

| 28 pieces of furniture | $C + S = 28$ |
| 100 legs total | $4C + 3S = 100$ |

You can use your calculator to find a common solution for the two equations. First translate the equations into Y= form.

| $x + y = 28$ | or | $y = 28 - x$ |
| $4x + 3y = 100$ | or | $y = \frac{100 - 4x}{3}$ |

Enter the first equation in Y1 and the second in Y2. The common solution for both equations is the point where the lines intersect. Press $\boxed{\text{TRACE}}$ and see if you can find the point of intersection.

It is often difficult to find the exact value of the common solution using the TRACE key. There are several other ways to get an exact value for the point of intersection.

Press $\boxed{\text{2nd}}$ [TABLE]. The calculator will display a table of values. The common solution for the two equations is the x-value for which Y1 and Y2 are the same. Can you find the common solution using the table? In cases where the common solution is not an integer, you may need to press $\boxed{\text{2nd}}$ [TblSet] and adjust the value for ΔTbl. Smaller and smaller values for ΔTbl will let you observe smaller and smaller intervals for the x-value.

The calculator can calculate the point of intersection of two lines directly. Press $\boxed{\text{2nd}}$ [CALC]. A menu appears showing many things the calculator can do for you. Select 5 and the calculator will find the coordinates of the point of intersection. The calculator will ask "First curve?" Use the up or down arrow to place the cursor on one of the lines, and press $\boxed{\text{ENTER}}$. Then the calculator will move the cursor to the other line and ask for the second curve. Press $\boxed{\text{ENTER}}$ again. Now the calculator will ask for a guess. Use the right or left arrow to move the cursor near to the point of intersection (you don't have to be precise) and press $\boxed{\text{ENTER}}$. The calculator will give you the exact coordinates of the point of intersection. How many chairs and stools should Fiona make?

There are several other nifty things your calculator can do from the CALC menu. Follow along with your calculator in hand to explore them.

❏ **1:value** If you select 1, the calculator will ask you for an *x*-value and then give you the corresponding *y*-value. You can use the up or down arrow to change equations, and you can use the right or left arrow to change the value of *x*. If Fiona decided to make 10 stools, how many chairs would she be able to make with the leftover legs? In this situation, you only need the equation in Y2. (You can turn off the equation in Y1 by highlighting the = sign and pressing ENTER.) From the CALC menu, select 1:value. Then enter 10. The calculator will respond with the number of chairs Fiona can make.

❏ **2:zero** (**root** on the TI-82) This function finds the *x*-value where a function is equal to zero. When you select 2, the calculator will ask you for a Left Bound and Right Bound. It is asking, "In what window do you want to look for a root?" Place the cursor on a point to the left of where you think there may be a root and press ENTER. Then move the cursor to the right of where you think the root may be and press ENTER again. Now the calculator will ask you for a guess. Place the cursor close to where you think the root is and press ENTER. The calculator will give you the *x*-value of the root. If there is no root in the area you ask the calculator to search, it will give you an error message. If Fiona wanted to find out how many chairs to make if she made no stools, she could use this function on the equation in Y2. Try it and see how it works.

❏ **3:minimum** and **4:maximum** These work very similarly to the zero/root function. The calculator will find the highest or lowest *y*-values in a neighborhood that you choose. Enter the equation $y = x^3 + 2x^2 - 10x - 15$ in Y3, and press GRAPH. Adjust the window until you have a good view of the graph.

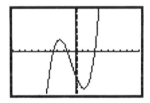

From the CALC menu select 3, and specify the neighborhood around the low point of the graph in Quadrant IV to find the low point of the function there. This is called a *local minimum*, because it is not the lowest value of the function, but a minimum within a given neighborhood. Select 4 to find the *local maximum* in Quadrant II.

Practice Problems

1. Fiona did some spring cleaning and, to her great surprise, she discovered 48 more legs in a box in her workshop. She has figured that with some help from her friend Phoebe, they can make a total of 44 chairs and stools. How many chairs and stools should Fiona and Phoebe make so they won't waste any legs?
2. Use a method different from the one you used in Problem 1 to solve the same problem. Write a few sentences explaining which method you prefer and why.
3. Enter the equation $y = x^3 + 3x^2 - 4x - 12$ in Y1 and graph it. Adjust the window so you have a good view of the curve. Make a sketch of the curve.
   a. Find the zeros/roots of the equation.
   b. Find the value of the equation when $x = {}^-2.5$.

More Than Graphs, Revised Edition • ©2004 Key Curriculum Press

   c. Find the local minimum in Quadrant IV.

   d. Find the local maximum in Quadrant II.

     Find the common solution(s) for each set of equations. If the equation is not in Y= form, then solve for y first.

4. $3y - 2x = 4$

   $y = {}^{-}0.75x + 10$

5. $2x + 2y = {}^{-}21$

   $xy = 20$

6. $y = \sqrt{x + 1}$

   $y = x$

7. $y = \cos x$

   $y = \sin x$

   Note: The sine and cosine are trigonometric functions. You will see more of them in geometry and advanced algebra. In order to get a nice window, choose ZoomStat.

Extension Problem

A small boy, ignoring his mother's sage advice, chooses to go hiking across a railroad trestle that is about 1 mile long. He is 1/4 the distance across the trestle when he hears a train whistle, apparently as it has just exited a tunnel. He knows that trains travel at about 50 miles/hour and the tunnel is 1 mile from where he started walking across the trestle. His top speed is 10 miles/hour. At this moment, he believes he is very capable of running that fast. Which way should he run? Hint: Let Y1 equal a function reflecting the boy's speed. Evaluate x at the moment the train reaches the near end of the trestle and the moment the train reaches the far end of the trestle.

Common Solutions

Objective: To use the CALC feature to find common or multiple solutions to a system of equations

Materials needed: TI-82, TI-83, or TI-83 Plus graphing calculator

Appropriate level: Algebra and pre-algebra

Time involved: One hour or class period

Preparation: Experience with graphing lines and finding a point of intersection

This activity introduces students to a variety of features of the calculator, which they may not even realize are there.

My students enjoyed using these new features to further explore functions. Prior to this, they had asked questions such as, "What is a root?", "What do sin and cos mean?", and "How can there be a maximum?" One of the side benefits of this activity is that it lets students explore some nonlinear functions. While working on this activity, my students became quite interested in some of the curious shapes they could make using different types of functions.

Solutions

Practice Problems

1. (16, 28) 16 chairs and 28 stools
2. Answers will vary.
3. a. (−3, 0), (−2, 0), and (2, 0)
   b. 1.125
   c. (.5275, −13.128)
   d. (−2.528, 1.128)
4. (4.235, 6.823)
5. (−8, −2.5) and (−2.5, −8)
6. (1.618, 1.618)
7. (45, .7071)

Extension Problem

At 50 miles/hour the train will be at the near end of the trestle in 1 minute and 12 seconds. In that time, the boy can run 0.2 mile. He will not beat the train to the near end of the trestle, which is 0.25 mile away. The train will be at the far end of the trestle in 2 minutes and 24 seconds. In that time, he will be able to run 0.4 mile. He will not beat the train to the far end, either. It is 0.75 mile away. He had better think of something else quickly!

The Search for π

Using Geometric Probability to Approximate π

Setting the Stage

The number π is an interesting number to explore. Your graphing calculator has the value of π built in. However, you might be curious as to how mathematicians were able to compute the value of π before these calculators were available. This activity explores a method for approximating the value of π using a geometric probability model.

The Activity

First you will need to work with a team of classmates to collect some data.

Construct a target like the one shown. The side length of the large square should be about 2 feet.

Each team member should stand about 10 feet from the target and toss 10 chips, trying to land somewhere on the large square, not necessarily in the circle.

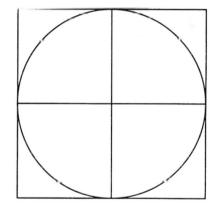

After all team members have thrown their chips, record the following data.

How many chips are inside the circle?
How many chips landed on the target?

Repeat this experiment at least five times.

Trial Number	Chips in the Circle	Chips on the Target
1		
2		
3		
4		
5		
Total		

Now answer these questions:

If the length of the side of the square target is 1 unit, what is the area of the square? _____
What is the area of the circle in terms of π? _____
What is the ratio of the area of the circle to the area of the square? _____

Now use this ratio and the data you collected to estimate the value of π.

$$\frac{\text{area of the circle}}{\text{area of the square}} = \frac{\text{total number of chips in the circle}}{\text{total number of chips on the target}}$$

Solve the proportion for π and you have an approximation of its value. Do this and compare your answer to the calculator value for π.

What could you do so that your results would be closer to π? In the Practice Problems you will explore several options.

Practice Problems

1. One way to improve the accuracy of the results is to collect more samples. Collect the data from other groups in your class and record it in the table below.

Group Number	Chips in the Circle	Chips on the Target
Total		

Use the proportion to compute the value of π again. Compare this value to the value you got using only the data from your group. Compare this value to the calculator value for π. Write a sentence or two describing your results.

2. By using a calculator program, you can generate a lot of data in a short period of time. Below are programs that simulate throwing darts at a target.

TI-82/TI-83 Program

```
PROGRAM:DARTS
ClrDraw:ClrHome
PlotsOff
-1.5→Xmin:1.5→Xmax:AxesOff
-1→Ymin:1→Ymax:0 Yscl
Input "HOW MANY DARTS?",A
Line(-1,1,1,1)
Line(1,1,1,-1)
Line(1,-1,-1,-1)
Line(-1,-1,-1,1)
Line(0,-1,0,1)
Line(1,0,-1,0)
Circle(0,0,1)
0→P
For(B,1,A)
2rand-1→X
2rand-1→Y
Pt-On(X,Y)
If X²+Y²≤1
P+1→P
Text(30,5,B)
End
P/A*4→K
Text(30,80,K)
```

TI-73 Program

```
PROGRAM:DARTS
ClrScreen
PlotsOff
-1.5 Xmin:1.5→Xmax:AxesOff
-1 Ymin:1→Ymax:0 Yscl
Input "HOW MANY DARTS?",A
Line(-1,1,1,1)
Line(1,1,1,-1)
Line(1,-1,-1,-1)
Line(-1,-1,-1,1)
Line(0,-1,0,1)
Line(1,0,-1,0)
Circle(0,0,1)
0→P
For(B,1,A)
2rand-1→X
2rand-1→Y
Pt-On(X,Y)
If X²+Y²≤1
P+1→P
Text(30,5,B)
End
P/A*4→K
Text(30,80,K)
```

When you execute the program, it will ask you for the number of darts. When you press ENTER, the calculator will display the target and start "throwing" darts. On the left-hand side of the calculator screen, you will see a running tally of the number of darts thrown. After all the darts are thrown, the calculator will compute the value of π using the same proportion you used in the activity. The result will be displayed on the right-hand side of the screen.

Try this experiment several times using a different number of darts each time. Make a table to record your results. Write a paragraph describing what you tried and your results.

3. Do you think the size of the chip or the size of the target could affect the accuracy of your results? Experiment with changing one or the other and see what effect it has on your approximation of π. Write a paragraph describing your experiment and your results.

Extension Problems

1. Letting the Calculator Find π

   Letting the calculator find π is not the same as pushing the π key. Pushing the π key just retrieves a value that was burned into the computer chips when the calculator was made. One way that has been used to approximate irrational numbers has been to find a series that approach those numbers as you add more terms. You can approximate π by evaluating a fairly simple series. This series is named after Gottfried Wilhelm Leibniz, 1646–1716, a German philosopher and mathematician, though it was discovered by James Gregory, 1638–1675, a Scottish mathematician. As you add more terms to the computation, your approximation will get closer to the real value for π.

   $$\frac{\pi}{4} = 1 - \frac{1}{3} + \frac{1}{5} - \frac{1}{7} + \frac{1}{9} - \cdots$$

   One way of doing this is to use the ANS function. Press 1, then ENTER. Now when you press an operation sign, ANS will appear on the screen. So if you want to subtract 1/3 from the previous result, 1, all you have to do is press ⁻1/3 ENTER. Next press +1/5 ENTER. As you continue to follow the pattern in the series, your result will get closer and closer to $\frac{\pi}{4}$.

   The calculator value for $\frac{\pi}{4}$ is 0.7853981634. How many terms will it take using this series to find the value of $\frac{\pi}{4}$ accurate to two decimal places? _____

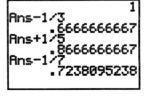

2. [Doing the Same Thing] in Seq mode (TI-82 and TI-83 only)

   $$\begin{cases} 1 & \text{if } n = 1 \\ \text{ANS} - \left((-1)^n / (2^n - 1)\right) & \text{if } n > 1 \end{cases}$$

   Another way of expressing this series is using what is called *recursive notation*. The variable n represents the number of the term. When $n = 1$, the value of the first term is 1. When $n = 2$, the value of the second term is

   $$\text{the first term} - \frac{(-1)^2}{2 \cdot 2 - 1} = 1 - \frac{1}{3}$$

   Likewise, for the third term, you would compute

   $$\text{the second term} - \frac{(-1)^3}{2 \cdot 3 - 1} = 0.66666666667 + \frac{1}{5}$$

   You can watch this unfold using the Sequence mode on the TI-82 and TI-83. First, be sure to disable or erase all Y= functions and plots. Then change the MODE settings from Functions to Sequence. Change the other settings to those shown on the next page.

TI-83 Screens

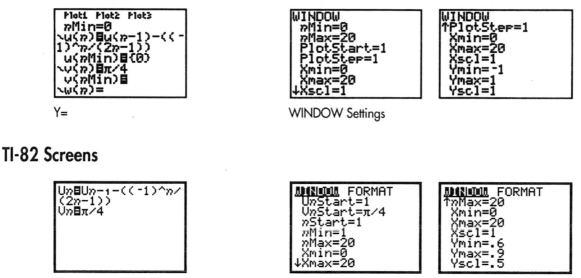

| Y= | WINDOW Settings | |

TI-82 Screens

| Y= | WINDOW Settings | |

Press $\boxed{\text{2nd}}$ [TABLE] to see the table of values calculated by the calculator.

Press $\boxed{\text{GRAPH}}$ to see the path the calculator is taking as it searches for the value of π.

Note: U_{n-1} acts as an accumulator, recursively collecting the new values of U_n. V_n stays constant as a reference point. By increasing Xmax and nMax, you can explore what happens as the calculator computes values closer and closer to $\frac{\pi}{4}$.

The Search for π

Objective: To learn about different methods for approximating π

Materials needed: TI-82, TI-83, or TI-83 Plus graphing calculator for parametrics (otherwise, a TI-73 will work), butcher paper, meter sticks, string or a large compass, chips or pennies to be tossed

Appropriate level: Algebra and pre-algebra

Time involved: One hour or class period

Preparation: Experience with solving proportions

I've always found π to be a very mysterious concept. With these activities, I try to encourage students to share in the search for the real value of π.

The activity introduces students to the concept of geometric probability, which is useful in simulating many real-life situations. In this case they use it to find an approximate value for π, working with the area of a circle rather than the more traditional comparison of the ratio of the circumference to the diameter. This is actually done in another activity, *Polygon π*.

In the Extension Problems, students are introduced to a series that is used to approximate π. It is relatively easy to generate partial sums on the calculator using a very simple

routine. This routine is then translated into a formula so they can experience using the sequence mode on the TI-82 and TI-83 calculators. Students may need help in understanding the formula used here. Even if students do only Extension Problem 1, it would be worthwhile to show them the graph generated in Extension Problem 2 as it provides a very visual representation of what is happening as the calculator computes values closer and closer to $\frac{\pi}{4}$.

You might want to introduce students to the Indpnt:Auto Ask function in the TblSet window. This function will allow them to access one term in the sequence. Select Ask, and then press `2nd` [TABLE]. Enter the term number you want to see, and the calculator will calculate it.

Solutions

Activity

The area of the square is 1 square unit.
The area of the circle is $\frac{\pi}{4}$ square units.
The ratio of the area of the circle to the area of the square is $\frac{\pi}{4}$.

Practice Problems

Answers will vary.

Extension Problems

The displayed calculator value for $\frac{\pi}{4}$ is 0.7853981634.
$1 - \frac{1}{3} + \frac{1}{5} \ldots - \frac{1}{95}$ is the first sum that is accurate to two decimal places.

Polygon π

Using Successive Approximations to Find the Value of π

Setting the Stage

From the time of the ancient Greeks until the present day, mathematicians have been intrigued by the problem of computing closer and closer approximations for the value of π, which is defined to be the ratio of the circumference to the length of the diameter for any circle. However, it's difficult to measure a circumference and a diameter accurately enough to obtain a very accurate value for π. However, you can find a fairly accurate value for π by looking at the relationship between the perimeter of a regular polygon and the length of its longest diagonal.

As you look at polygons with more and more sides, you will be looking at figures that more closely resemble a circle than a polygon, so this ratio will get closer and closer to the ratio of the circumference of a circle to its diameter.

The Activity

First you will need to enter the following program, which will draw an even-sided regular polygon built upon a diagonal of the length you specify.

TI-82/TI-83 Program

```
PROGRAM:PI
Param:Degree
AxesOff:PlotsOff:FnOff:GridOff
"Acos(T)"→X₁ᴛ
"Asin(T)"→Y₁ᴛ
0→Tmin:360→Tmax:
⁻18→Xmin:18→Xmax:3→Xscl
⁻12→Ymin:12→Ymax:3→Yscl
Repeat fPart(N/2)=0 and N>0 and A>0 and A≤10
ClrHome:Disp "EVEN NUMBER"
Input "OF SIDES?",N
Disp "LEN OF DIAGONAL"
Input "(UP TO 20)?",B
B/2→A
End
360/N→Tstep
DispGraph
```

Experiment with the program a few times until you are comfortable with the way it operates. To run the program again and draw a new polygon, press CLEAR twice and then ENTER.

Now you can start to gather data about regular polygons. Run the program. Enter 4 for the number of sides and 20 for the diagonal. After the calculator draws a square (oriented to look like a diamond), press TRACE. You should see the cursor flashing on the corner farthest to the right. The T-value of 0 indicates that the point is located 0 degrees from due east. The y-coordinate of this first point will be 0 for any polygon, and the x-coordinate will be half of the diagonal length you entered. Can you explain why this happens? The coordinates of this point have already been entered into the table in the Practice Problems.

Next, press the right arrow to move to the next corner around the square. Since you are looking at a 4-sided figure, T indicates you are now $\frac{1}{4}$ of the way around the figure, or at an angle of 90 degrees from due east. The coordinates of this point, (0, 10), have been entered into the table for you. Press CLEAR twice and use the calculator screen to compute the length of this side, using the distance formula. Enter this answer into the appropriate column for the length of this side. Multiply this entry by N, the number of sides (in this case, 4). This gives the perimeter of the polygon, which should be entered in the perimeter column of the table. Finally, take the ratio of the distance all the way around to the distance across (P/D) and enter this value into the last column.

Practice Problems

Gather and record the data about different polygons in this table. Then use this data to compute the ratio of P/D for each polygon. The most efficient way to do this is to creatively use the STAT feature of your calculator.

First use the program π to draw a polygon for each row of the table. Use the TRACE feature to find the coordinates of two consecutive vertices of each polygon, and record each pair of coordinates in the appropriate column. Do this for each polygon listed in the table, without stopping to calculate the side lengths, perimeters, or ratios. Be sure to choose different diagonal lengths when the number of sides is the same.

When you have completed the table, press STAT EDIT and enter all the x-coordinates of the first points in L1 and the corresponding y-coordinates in L2, the x-coordinates of the second points in L3 and the corresponding y-coordinates in L4. You can now take advantage of the power of your calculator by entering the distance formula in L5. See if you can figure out how to do this using L1, L2, L3, and L4 rather than x_1, x_2, y_1, and y_2.

You can also use the STAT feature to calculate the perimeter and P/D for each polygon. Because there are only six lists available in the calculator, you will need to clear at least the first four lists to create space. This isn't a problem because you won't need the coordinates again. Enter the number of sides of each polygon in L1, and the length of each diagonal in L2. Then you can use the calculator to compute the length of the perimeter in L3 and the ratio P/D in L4.

Record your calculations in the table.

Trial Number (N)	Number of Sides (N)	Length of Diagonal (D)	First Point (X, Y)	Second Point (X, Y)	Length of Side (S)	Length of Perimeter (P = N · S)	P/D
1							
2							
3							
4							
5							
6							
7							
8							
9							
10							
11							
12							
13							
14							
15							

1. Examine the results of your computations for the squares. What do you notice about the ratios entered in the last column? Can you explain your finding? Write a paragraph explaining this phenomenon. Include in it words like *proportional* and the completion of this sentence: "Since all squares are similar to all other squares and are thus scale models of each other, the perimeter of any square is always _____ times the diagonal distance across that square."
2. Experiment next with hexagons, then octagons, decagons, and so on. What do you notice about the values in the last column as you increase the number of sides? Is there a value that these seem to approach?
3. Do you see why the program uses only even-sided regular polygons? What difficulty would you run into if you tried this with triangles or pentagons?
4. Using what you have learned, write a paragraph explaining the relationship between the perimeter of a circle (known as its circumference) and its diagonal (or diameter).

Extension Problem

Your calculator is pretty smart. When you trace, the last x- and y-values are automatically stored in the calculator. If you return to the Home screen after tracing, you can retrieve these values by pressing ⟨X,T,Θ,n⟩ ⟨ENTER⟩ or ⟨ALPHA⟩ [Y] ⟨ENTER⟩ ⟨2nd⟩. You can automate the process of finding the length of a side and the perimeter by writing a program that uses these stored values. When your cursor is on the first vertex, return to the Home screen by pressing ⟨CLEAR⟩ twice, and store the *x*- and *y*-values in another location, say, G and H. You can do this by pressing ⟨X,T,Θ,n⟩ ⟨STO►⟩ ⟨ALPHA⟩ [G] ⟨ENTER⟩ and ⟨ALPHA⟩ [Y] ⟨STO►⟩ ⟨ALPHA⟩ [H] ⟨ENTER⟩. Then press ⟨GRAPH⟩ ⟨TRACE⟩ and move to the next vertex. Return to the Home screen. The two points that you want to find the distance between are (G, H) and (X, Y). You could do this by using the distance formula with the variables G, H, X, and Y.

Now write a short program that will compute the length of the side, the perimeter, and the ratio between the perimeter and the length of the diagonal. (This value is stored in B in the original program.) You might even be able to figure out a way to automatically store these values in the list.

More Than Graphs, Revised Edition • ©2004 Key Curriculum Press

Polygon π

Objective:	To learn about different methods for approximating π
Materials needed:	TI-82, TI-83, or TI-83 Plus graphing calculator
Appropriate level:	Algebra and pre-algebra
Time involved:	One hour or class period
Preparation:	Experience with the distance formula

In this activity, students use the idea that as the number of sides of a regular polygon increases, the polygon becomes more circlelike and the ratio of its perimeter to the length of its longest diagonals approaches the ratio of the circumference to the diameter in a circle. The program allows them to draw any even-sided polygon based on the length of its diagonal. They can then trace to find the coordinates of two adjacent vertices and use the distance formula to find the length of a side. Then they are asked to compute the ratio of the perimeter to the length of the diagonal.

Students will investigate another interesting feature of the calculator in the Extension Problem. When you return to the Home screen after tracing, the last x- and y-values are automatically stored. These values can be retrieved and used for computation on the Home screen or in a program. If some of your students are programmers, you might want to suggest that they look at the Extension Problem before completing the table in the Practice Problem.

Solutions

Practice Problems

1. $\sqrt{2}$ or ≈ 1.414
2. The values in the last column seem to approach π.
3. The diagonals are not all the same length.
4. The ratio of the circumference to the diameter in any circle is approximately 3.14.

Extension Problem

An example of a possible program for calculating the length of a side, the perimeter, and the ratio. This program does not store the values to a list.

TI-82/TI-83 Program

```
PROGRAM:DISTANCE
√((G–X)²+(H–Y)²)→E
Disp E
N*E→F
Disp F
Disp F/B
```

Great Gonzo, the Human Cannonball

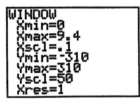

Constructing a Mathematical Simulation for a Falling Body

Setting the Stage

Great Gonzo, the human cannonball, defies death nightly, and in matinees on weekends, by being fired straight up out of a circus cannon at a muzzle velocity of 100 feet per second. His brief flight into the stratosphere is carefully planned to bring him safely back to earth, landing in a net of nylon webbing that has been set up by a crack crew of efficient circus employees during the flight. Gonzo has recently fired his manager, and he has hired you to keep him safe from all harm. Your job is to model his flight mathematically and ensure that everything is set up to keep Gonzo from going "splat!"

The Activity

First you need to analyze the problem and make some assumptions.

Great Gonzo's flight is actually the result of two forces—the upward propulsion caused by his being fired from the cannon, and the downward force of gravity.

The distance, d, traveled by an object moving at a constant velocity, V_0, is $d = V_0t$, where t indicates time.

The distance, d, traveled by an accelerating object is $d = 0.5\,at^2$, where a is the acceleration and t is time.

Assume that all objects on earth, not subject to air resistance, will fall at an acceleration of 32 ft/sec^2.

Gonzo's flight can be studied with the help of a mathematical model. You will need three functions: one for the cannon, one for gravity, and one for the combined interaction of both. First, set up a window for the graph.

```
WINDOW
 Xmin=0
 Xmax=9.4
 ▵X=.1
 Xscl=1
 Ymin=-310
 Ymax=310
 Yscl=50
```
TI-73

```
WINDOW
 Xmin=0
 Xmax=9.4
 Xscl=.1
 Ymin=-310
 Ymax=310
 Yscl=50
 Xres=1
```
TI-82/TI-83

154

Define Y1 to be the distance traveled upward as a result of the muzzle velocity.

Enter Y1 = 100x.

Make a graph of the function, and sketch it here.

Define Y2 as the distance traveled downward as a result of the acceleration due to gravity.

Enter Y2 = ⁻0.5 · 32x².

Make a graph of this function, and sketch it here.

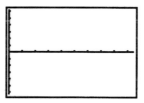

In each case, what does the line y = 0 represent?

Now create a new function, Y3, by adding Y1 and Y2. Position the cursor in Y3. On the TI-83, press VARS Y-VARS. (This is 2nd [Y-VARS] on the TI-82 and 2nd [VARS] 2 on the TI-73.) Select 1: Function and enter the number of the function you want to choose, in this case 1 for Y1.

$$Y3 = Y1 + Y2$$

Turn off Y1 and Y2 without erasing them by highlighting the = sign and pressing ENTER.

Press GRAPH to see Gonzo's flight. Sketch the graph below.

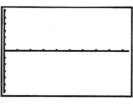

Press MODE and highlight Simul rather than Sequential. This will let you see all three equations graphed simultaneously. Press Y= and turn on all three equations by highlighting each equal sign and pressing GRAPH. (If you want to see an "instant replay," turn off one of the functions and then turn it back on again.) Describe how the graph of Y3 is affected by the graphs of Y1 and Y2.

Practice Problems

Press ⟨ 2nd ⟩ [TABLE] to further examine Gonzo's flight. Use the information in the table to answer these important questions concerning Gonzo's safety.

1. How tall does the tent need to be?
2. How long do the clowns have to set up the net?
3. The head clown explains that even working at maximum speed, the clowns will need 5 seconds to unroll the net.
   a. Is this enough time?
   b. What advice would you give Gonzo about altering his initial velocity to ensure that the net will be rolled out in time?
   c. How high will Gonzo travel with this new velocity?
4. Great Gonzo complains that too much gunpowder singes his mustache and orders the crew to use a charge that propels him at a muzzle velocity of 50 ft/sec. What will be the altitude and duration of Great Gonzo's final flight?

Extension Problems

1. Hortense, the high diver, has a dramatic act in which she pretends to dive off a high platform into a little bitty glass of water. What really happens is that at the very last second, a team of clowns appears with a safety net (one of those fire department things with the bull's eye on it) to catch Hortense. Hortense jumps off the platform, which is 40 feet high, at an upward velocity of 25 ft/sec^2. Gravity will affect Hortense just as it did Gonzo at a rate of -16 ft/sec. Enter two equations into your calculator and use them to model Hortense's flight. As Hortense's manager, how much time would you allow the clowns to get the net in place?
2. Zelda, the knife thrower, must throw each blade hard enough that it will drop less than 3 inches as it travels on its way toward her partner, Zeppo. The distance between Zeppo and Zelda is 20 feet.
   a. Use the equation for the effect of gravity from the activity to determine how long it will take the blade to fall the 3 inches after it is released.
   b. At what speed, in feet per second, must Zelda throw the knife for it to travel the 20 feet in that time?
   c. What do you think Zelda should do to compensate for the 3-foot drop?
3. Write a story about a circus performer whose act will be affected by gravity. Create an equation for his or her act, and use the calculator to model the performance. As this performer's manager, specify any restrictions that may affect his or her performance, such as height of tent, time, and so on.

Great Gonzo, the Human Cannonball

Objective: To construct a mathematical simulation for a falling body
Materials needed: TI-73, TI-82, TI-83, or TI-83 Plus graphing calculator
Appropriate level: Algebra and pre-algebra
Time involved: One hour or class period
Preparation: Familiarity with the terms *velocity* and *acceleration*

Great Gonzo is a fun story to tell. Some students have seen circus performers do similar feats; other students just enjoy the insights of learning how the tug-of-war between upward forces and gravity works. Be sure to talk about gravity a lot, because it is a very mysterious force for young people.

An interesting anecdote is that when we were discussing this lesson, I pointed out that the acceleration of gravity here would be 32 ft/sec², but in Canada it would be 9.8 m/sec². One of my students wanted to know why there was more gravity here than in Canada. Was it because it was closer to the North Pole? Hmmmm. . . . I wasn't ready for that one.

A good discussion question for this lesson is, "When is a mathematical simulation a superior method to study experimental conditions?"

Solutions

Practice Problems

1. 156.24 feet
2. 6.2 seconds
3. a. Yes, but it is close!
   b. Answers will vary.
   c. Answers will vary.
4. His altitude will be 39.04 feet, and his flight will take 3.12 seconds.

Extension Problems

1. Equations for Hortense's flight: $Y_1 = 40 + 25x$, $Y_2 = -16x^2$. The clowns have about 2.34 seconds.
2. Note that for this problem, you have to either solve for a change of 0.25 foot or change the equation to $Y_2 = -0.5 \cdot 32 \cdot 12x^2$ to compensate for inches.
   a. It will take the blade 0.125 seconds to fall the 3 inches.
   b. 160 feet/second
   c. Aim up!
3. Answers will vary.

Random Numbers

Using the Calculator to Generate Random Numbers

Setting the Stage

Most video-type games involve a variety of
rewards or penalties that appear after your
encounter with an obstacle. If these obstacles
appeared at the same place or time within a
program every time you played the game,
you would quickly lose interest in playing.
The unpredictability of these obstacles is
produced by random numbers generated
inside the program. These random numbers
can control the difficulty level, the location
of obstacles, any time constraints, and the
reward or penalty.

The Activity

There are several ways you can generate random numbers on your calculator. The easiest way
is directly from the Home screen. To do this, press [MATH] PRB [1]. Each time you press
[ENTER], a random number will appear on the screen. Do this now. Generate at least ten
random numbers by pressing [ENTER] after each one. Describe the range of the numbers
generated. What do you think the smallest possible number is? the largest possible number?

If you want to generate a list of random numbers that are between 0 and 9, all you have to do
is to slightly modify the command you entered before. Do the same series of keystrokes, but
this time enter rand · 10. Press [ENTER], and verify that the numbers are now between 0 and 9.

If you want to generate a sequence of whole numbers, there are two ways. For one way, all
you have to do is add one more part to the command. Press [MATH] NUM iPart (10 · [MATH]
PRB [1]). What you'll see on the Home screen is iPart (10*rand). Now each time you press
[ENTER], you will see a whole number. The iPart command displays the integer part of the
number (the part of the number before the decimal point). If you should want to start over
and generate a new sequence of numbers, all you have to do is press [CLEAR]. Press [ENTER]
and you're ready to generate.

An even easier way to do this on the TI-73 and TI-83 is to press [MATH] PRB, select
randInt(, and enter "0,9". Each time the [ENTER] key is pressed, a value between 0 and 9 will
appear on the screen.

Practice Problems

Random Number Game

In this game you will be competing with members of your group. You will all be working on the same problem at the same time. Your group will use one calculator to generate random numbers, one at a time. Each time a random number is generated, you should write it in one of the boxes of the problem your group is working on. Once you have placed a number in a box, you can't erase it and move it to another box. You must write in each number as it is generated (no passes). When you have filled in all the boxes for a problem, calculate your answer. When each group member has completed the calculation, compare answers to determine who receives a point. The group member with the best answer scores one point. Then proceed to the next problem.

Note: Remember that 0 can never be used as the divisor in a division problem.

Fill in each box so you will get the largest possible answer.

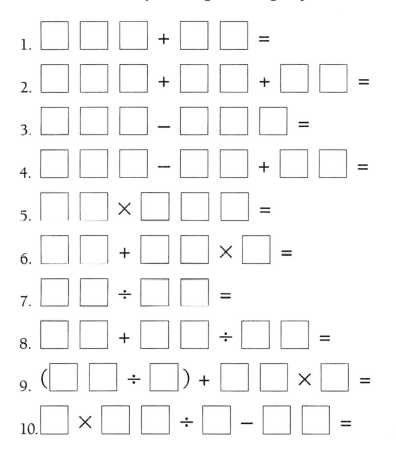

1. ☐☐☐ + ☐☐ =

2. ☐☐☐ + ☐☐ + ☐☐ =

3. ☐☐☐ − ☐☐☐ =

4. ☐☐☐ − ☐☐ + ☐☐ =

5. ☐☐ × ☐☐☐ =

6. ☐☐ + ☐☐ × ☐ =

7. ☐☐ ÷ ☐☐ =

8. ☐☐ + ☐☐ ÷ ☐☐ =

9. (☐☐ ÷ ☐) + ☐☐ × ☐ =

10. ☐ × ☐☐ ÷ ☐ − ☐☐ =

Now, do these same problems to find the smallest possible answer:

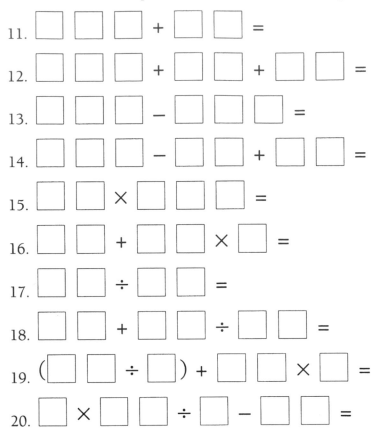

11. $\square\square\square + \square\square =$

12. $\square\square\square + \square\square + \square\square =$

13. $\square\square\square - \square\square\square =$

14. $\square\square\square - \square\square + \square\square =$

15. $\square\square \times \square\square\square =$

16. $\square\square + \square\square \times \square =$

17. $\square\square \div \square\square =$

18. $\square\square + \square\square \div \square\square =$

19. $(\square\square \div \square) + \square\square \times \square =$

20. $\square \times \square\square \div \square - \square\square =$

Extension Problems

1. Invent your own random number game. Write a description of your game including the rules. Play your game at least five times with a friend and/or someone at home. Write a report explaining how well your game worked. Was it fun? Was it fair? Did people enjoy playing the game?

2. Experiment with the miniprogram. See if you can make it simulate rolling a die. Try making it roll two dice and find the sum. Have your program store these numbers in a list so you can look at them when the program has finished running. Make a histogram of the results.

More Than Graphs, Revised Edition • ©2004 Key Curriculum Press

Random Numbers

Objective: To use the calculator as a random number generator and to extend arithmetic skills in a group situation

Materials needed: TI-73, TI-82, TI-83, or TI-83 Plus graphing calculator

Appropriate level: Algebra and pre-algebra

Time involved: One hour or class period

Preparation: Arrange the class in groups

This is a very open-ended activity. The goal of the game is to place random numbers in the position of greatest advantage or least disadvantage. With experience students will develop strategies. After the class has played the game several times, or during several different class periods, ask students to discuss their strategies.

It's a good idea to have each student seed the random number generator on their calculator. If you don't do this, you increase the probability that the random number sequences generated by each student will be the same. To seed the generator, ask each student to enter the last four digits of their telephone number. Then press ⌊**STO►**⌋ ⌊**MATH**⌋ PRB ⌊**1**⌋ ⌊**ENTER**⌋. This does not need to be repeated any time you start a new random number activity. Once at the beginning of the year is all that is needed. This ensures that all of the calculators do not generate the same random numbers.

The command iPart (10rand) can be edited to create a variety of random-generated number sequences. By changing the part of the command in the parentheses, you can change the range of

the numbers being generated. If you want to generate five digits between 0 and 5, multiply rand by 5. By adding a number to the rand part of the command, you can change the range of the sequence. For example, iPart (10rand + 1) generates a sequence of numbers between 1 and 10 rather than 0 and 9. The possibilities are endless for you and your students if you want to further explore programming techniques. You can generate a list of numbers, store these numbers in a list, draw a histogram showing the distribution, and calculate percentages, all within the same program.

The TI-73 and TI-83 have a built-in randInt function (⌊**MATH**⌋ PRB) that allows you to directly enter the range of integers you want, and then the calculator automatically generates integers in that range.

You or your students can create many other games using the random number generator. You can also use the generator to simulate probability experiments or to generate data for a statistical analysis.

Solutions

Practice Problems

Answers will vary.

Extension Problems

Answers will vary.

Decaying M&Ms®

Exploring Nonlinear Regression Equations

Setting the Stage

A decay function is one in which the values decrease by a nonlinear, but still constant, factor. These functions are often used to model the decay of a radioactive element. The half-life of a substance is the time it takes to reduce its initial effectiveness by one-half. The half-life of plutonium is 24,360 years, which is why storing atomic waste from nuclear power plants poses such a long-term problem to the biosphere in which that waste is deposited.

The Activity

Fill a cup with M&Ms. Count them to determine the initial sample size (N). This will be the value at time $t = 0$. Enter this value in the table, and put the M&Ms back in the cup.

Shake the cup and pour out the M&Ms on the paper. Remove all the M&Ms with an m showing. Count the remaining M&Ms. This will be the value of N at $t = 1$. Enter this value in the table, and put the remaining M&Ms back in the cup.

Shake the cup and pour out the M&Ms on the paper. Remove all the M&Ms with an m showing. Count the remaining M&Ms again. This will be the value of N at $t = 2$. Enter this value in the table, and put the remaining M&Ms back in the cup.

Repeat this process until there are no longer any M&Ms with an m showing when you empty the cup.

Press [**STAT**] EDIT ([**LIST**] on the TI-73) and enter the values of t in L1 and the values of N in L2. Use [**STAT PLOT**] ([**PLOT**] on the TI-73) to create a broken-line graph of the data. Make a sketch of the graph you have created. Describe the shape of this decay function.

Use the calculator to calculate the linear regression equation. Press [**STAT**] CALC LinReg [L1], [L2] [**ENTER**] ([**2nd**] [**STAT**] CALC LinReg L1, L2 on the TI-73.) (The comma between L1 and L2 is a necessary keystroke.)

Linear regression $y =$ _____

Time	N
1	
2	
3	
4	
5	
6	
7	

© Mars, Inc.

More Than Graphs, Revised Edition • ©2004 Key Curriculum Press

Enter this equation as Y1. To do this easily, place the cursor in Y1 as if you were going to enter an equation. Then press [VARS] Statistics EQ RegEQ ([2nd] [VARS] Statistics EQ RegEQ for the TI-73) to graph the linear regression equation on top of your broken-line graph. How well does it fit?

Use the calculator to calculate the quadratic regression equation. Press [STAT] CALC QuadReg [L1], [L2] ([2nd] [STAT] CALC QuadReg L1, L2 on the TI-73).

Quadratic regression y = _____

Enter this equation as Y2. Place the cursor in Y2 as if you were going to enter an equation. Then press [VARS] Statistics EQ RegEQ. (Press [2nd] [VARS] Statistics EQ RegEQ on the TI-73.) Press [GRAPH] to graph the quadratic regression equation on top of your broken-line graph. How well does it fit?

Use the calculator to calculate the exponential regression equation. (Find ExpReg in the STAT CALC menu.) To avoid getting an error message, you will need to delete any entry in L2 in which $N = 0$. You will also need to delete the corresponding t-value in L1.

Exponential regression y = _____

Enter this equation as Y3, and graph it on top of your broken-line graph. How well does it fit?

Which regression equation best describes the M&Ms decay function?

Practice Problem

Repeat the experiment, but this time use Kraft® caramels and remove the ones with the K on top each time. Sketch a graph and write the equation for each regression equation. Which regression equation best describes the Kraft caramel decay function?

Extension Problem

Design an experiment in which one third of the population will disappear each time.

© Kraft Foods, Inc.

Decaying M&Ms®

Objective:	To use a graphing calculator to enhance a mathematical simulation
Materials needed:	TI-73, TI-82, TI-83, or TI-83 Plus graphing calculator, individual M&Ms packets, or a large quantity of M&Ms and some small paper cups
Appropriate level:	Algebra and pre-algebra
Time involved:	One hour or class period
Preparation:	Discussion of exponential functions and decay

In this activity, students have the opportunity to explore a variety of regressions that are not linear. This activity is always everyone's favorite for obvious reasons. A promise of candy or snacks is always good for keeping the interest level high. You should ask students to wash their hands before beginning this lesson and to use a clean sheet of paper, not the desktop, as a work surface.

For each function, y is the current number of candies, K represents the original number of candies, and x is the number of the trial.

For M&Ms, the decay function should be pretty close to $y = K(0.5)x$.

Solutions

Practice Problem

For the Kraft® caramels, the decay function should be close to $y = K(5/6)x$.

Extension Problem

Answers will vary.

© Kraft Foods, Inc. © Mars, Inc.

Matrices

Using Matrix Operations to Solve Two-Variable Systems

Setting the Stage

A **matrix** is an array, or grid of numbers arranged in rows and columns. It can be added, subtracted, multiplied, or divided by another matrix. Usually you don't learn about matrices until you are in an advanced algebra class, but with your calculator, you can solve multivariable equations quite easily if you learn how to use the calculator matrix operations. It may seem a little bit like math magic, but if you think about the explanation given below, you should be able to relate the method to what you know about solving equations.

Reviewing What You Know

When you solve a one-variable equation, you use inverse operations and the identity elements. Inverse operations are operations that "undo" an operation. The inverse operation of addition is subtraction, and the inverse operation of multiplication is division, or multiplying by the reciprocal. When you do an inverse operation, you get what is called an **identity element**. If you multiply a number by its inverse, you get 1. For example, $5 \cdot \frac{1}{5} = 1$. The number 1 is the identity element for multiplication, since any number multiplied by 1 is the number itself. If you add a number to its inverse, you get 0. For example, $5 + 5 = 0$. The number 0 is the identity element for addition, because if you add 0 to any number, the sum will be the number itself.

Example		General Case
$2x = 10$		$ax = 10$
$\frac{1}{2} \cdot 2x = \frac{1}{2} \cdot 10$	Multiply both sides of the equation by the reciprocal of the coefficient of the variable.	$a^{-1} \cdot x = a^{-1}b$ (One way to write the reciprocal of a is a^{-1}.)
$2x = 10$	The product of a number and its reciprocal is the identity, 1. ($\frac{1}{2} \cdot 2 = 1$)($a^{-1} \cdot a = 1$)	$1 \cdot x = a^{-1}b$
$x = 5$	One times any number is the number itself. ($1x = 1$)	$x = a^{-1}b$

Using Matrices to Solve a System of Equations

In matrix algebra this same concept is used to solve a system of equations.

Here is an example of a 2×2 matrix $\begin{bmatrix} 7 & 6 \\ -1 & -4 \end{bmatrix}$, a 1×2 matrix $[2 \ -1]$, and a 2×1 matrix $\begin{bmatrix} 6 \\ 11 \end{bmatrix}$.

When you refer to a matrix as being 2×1, that means it has 2 rows and 1 column. Each number in a matrix is called an *entry*.

Solving for multiple variables requires three matrices, one for the coefficients, one for the variables, and one for the constants. So a system of equations such as $\begin{matrix} 1x + 2y = 24 \\ 3x + {}^-4y = 2 \end{matrix}$ can be written using matrices like this: $\begin{bmatrix} 1 & 2 \\ 3 & -4 \end{bmatrix} \begin{bmatrix} x \\ y \end{bmatrix} = \begin{bmatrix} 24 \\ 2 \end{bmatrix}$.

Can you figure out where all the matrix entries come from?

You can write this as $[A] \ [x] = [B]$, where $[A]$ is the matrix of all coefficients, $[x]$ is the matrix of all variables, and $[B]$ is the matrix of all constants. To solve this matrix equation, you follow the same process as you do with equations.

$$[A] \ [x] = [B]$$

Multiply $[A]$ by its inverse. $\qquad [A]^{-1} \ [A] \ [x] = [A]^{-1} \ [B]$

But $[A^{-1}]$ is the identity, or 1, so $\qquad [x] = [A]^{-1} \ [B]$

This means the variable matrix $[x]$ can be found by multiplying $[A]^{-1}[B]$.

Now you can solve the system of equations $\begin{matrix} 1x + 2y = 24 \\ 3x + {}^-4y = 2 \end{matrix}$ using matrices.

In this example, $[A] = \begin{bmatrix} 1 & 2 \\ 3 & -4 \end{bmatrix}$. To enter this matrix in your calculator, press $\boxed{\text{MATRX}}$ ($\boxed{\text{2nd}}$

$[\ \text{MATRIX}\ ]$ on the TI-83 Plus) and use the right arrow to highlight EDIT. Press $\boxed{1}$ to select $[A]$. Use the arrow keys to move around the screen. Enter the dimensions 2×2, and input each value in $[A]$.

Select $\boxed{\text{MATRX}}$ ($\boxed{\text{2nd}}$ $[\ \text{MATRIX}\ ]$ on the TI-83 Plus) EDIT again and choose $[B]$. $[B]$ is a 2×1 matrix that holds the constants.

In this example $[B] = \begin{bmatrix} 24 \\ 2 \end{bmatrix}$. Enter the dimensions of $[B]$ and each of its entries. Press $\boxed{\text{2nd}}$ $[\ \text{QUIT}\ ]$ to leave the matrix editor.

Now calculate $[A]^{-1}[B]$. Press (MATRX) ((2nd) [MATRIX] on the TI-83 Plus) and notice that NAMES is highlighted. Press (1) to select [A] and press (x⁻¹). Now press (MATRX) ((2nd) [MATRIX] on the TI-83 Plus) (2) to select [B].

When you press (ENTER), the solution matrix [x] appears.

$$\begin{bmatrix} x \\ y \end{bmatrix} = \begin{bmatrix} 10 \\ 7 \end{bmatrix}$$, so the solution to the system of equations is (10, 7).

Practice Problems

Use matrix algebra to find the common solution to each pair of linear equations.

1. $x + y = 10$
   $x - y = 2$

2. $2x - y = 0$
   $^-x - y = 16$

3. $x + 3y = 3$
   $x + 2y = 12$

4. $x + y = 1$
   $3x - 2y = 16$

5. $3x - y = ^-7$
   $x + 4y = 6$

6. $4x - y = 5$
   $3x - y = ^-5000$

7. $3x - 9y = 6$
   $7x - y = 0$

8. $6x - 2y = 3$
   $5x - 15y = 0$

Extension Problems

Often, you will find that equations you want to solve are not in *standard notation*. The first step, before using matrix algebra to solve these equations, is to write them in the form $Ax + By = C$. In this form, the term with the *x*-value always comes first. Now you're ready to write the matrix equation.

Use matrices to solve these systems of equations.
1. $3y + 5x = 35$
   $197 = 4y - 7x$

2. $785 - 4x = 3y$
   $2x - 7y = ^-687$

3. $x = 3$
   $y - x - 2$

4. The power of matrices is that they can be used to solve a system of equations with many variables. You just have to be sure that the number of equations is equal to the number of variables! The system of equations

   $x + ^-y + z = 13$
   $2x - y - 2z = 4$ can be solved using the matrices $[A] = \begin{bmatrix} 1 & ^-1 & 1 \\ 2 & ^-1 & ^-2 \\ 1 & 2 & 6 \end{bmatrix}$, and $[B] = \begin{bmatrix} 13 \\ 4 \\ 13 \end{bmatrix}$.
   $x + 2y + 6z = 13$

   Solve this system using your calculator, the given matrices, and matrix algebra.
5. What happens when you try to solve this system of equations using matrices?
   $y = 2x + 7$ and $y = 2x - 5$
   Explain why it happens. You may want to use a graph in your explanation.

Matrices

Objective: To use matrix operations to solve two-variable systems of equations
Materials needed: TI-82, TI-83, or TI-83 Plus graphing calculator
Appropriate level: Algebra and pre-algebra
Time involved: One hour or class period
Preparation: Familiarity with inverse and identity elements

Although I don't use this lesson with my pre-algebra students, my first-year algebra students thought it was "just neat." They hadn't had any previous experience with matrix operations, and I think that part of the excitement was just exploring something new. Many of them had wondered what the MATRX key did on the calculator, but I waited to introduce them to matrices until they had learned something about systems of equations and intersecting lines.

Several of my students chose to create their own problems with three- and four-variable equations just to watch the machine solve them so they could check the answers. What made it more interesting to them was the discussion we had about visualizing three-dimensional graphs with x-, y-, and z-coordinates. It really sparked the imaginations of some students.

Solutions

Practice Problems

1. $(6, 4)$
2. $\left(\frac{-16}{3}, \frac{-32}{3}\right)$
3. $(30, -9)$
4. $(3.6, -2.6)$
5. $(-1.692, 1.923)$
6. $(5005, 20015)$
7. $(-0.1, m -0.7)$
8. $(-4.5, -15)$

Extension Problems

1. $(-731, 1230)$
2. $(101, 127)$
3. $(3, 1)$
4. $(4.2, 11, -2.2)$
5. When you try to solve this system using matrices, you get the error message "Err: Singular Matrix." This is because the matrix [A] is singular, which means it has no inverse. Graphing the lines gives a good picture of why there is no solution. The lines are parallel!

Projector

Exploring Some Ideas in Projective Geometry

Setting the Stage

The goal of artists during the Renaissance was the accurate depiction of the real world. Leonardo da Vinci believed that a painting must be an exact reproduction of reality, so he and other painters developed the theory of perspective. Leonardo regarded painting as a science because it reveals the reality in nature. For this reason, Leonardo believed painting to be superior to poetry, music, and even architecture. As a result of the development of perspective, a new branch of mathematics developed called **projective geometry**.

Projective geometry examines similar polygons that lie in different planes. If you draw lines through corresponding vertices of two similar polygons in different planes and extend these lines, they will all intersect in one point. This point of intersection is called the **point of projection**. If the two polygons are congruent, the lines will be parallel. In projective geometry, such lines are said to intersect at infinity.

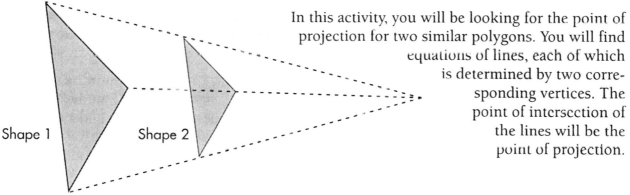

In this activity, you will be looking for the point of projection for two similar polygons. You will find equations of lines, each of which is determined by two corresponding vertices. The point of intersection of the lines will be the point of projection.

Shape 1   Shape 2

The Activity

Follow the steps below to find the point of projection defined by these two triangles.

Triangle 1	Triangle 2
A1 = (1, 4)	B1 = (5, 5)
A2 = (5, 3)	B2 = (13, 3)
A3 = (3, 7)	B3 = (9, 11)

Turn the GridOn in [2nd] FORMAT ([WINDOW] FORMAT on the TI-82) and enter these
WINDOW settings: [⁻4, 14.8, 2, 0, 12.4, 2, 1]. Press [GRAPH].

Use the LINE function to draw the
triangles directly on the Home
screen. This is [2nd] [DRAW] [2]
on the TI-82 and TI-83, and just
[DRAW] [2] on the TI-73. Once you
have selected this function from the
graph screen, you can continue to
draw lines without reselecting the
function. The ENTER key acts as a toggle switch turning the pen on and off. Press [ENTER]
when you want to start drawing a segment and press it again when you've finished drawing
the line. This means that you will press [ENTER] twice each time you are at a vertex of your
polygon. When your triangles are drawn, it's a good idea to store the picture so you won't
have to draw it again later. Do this by selecting STO from the DRAW
menu, and then choose picture number 1–6 (1–3 on the TI-73). (Be
sure you do this, because your picture will disappear when you start
graphing your line functions from Y=.)

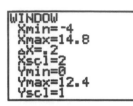

TI-73 Window (ΔX is a calculated
value and is not entered)

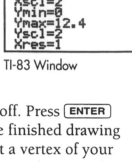

TI-83 Window

Use the LINE function again to draw three lines so that each one
passes through a pair of corresponding vertices. The easiest way to do
this is to position the cursor on a vertex, press [ENTER], and move the
cursor as far to the left or right as you can. Then move the line up or down using the arrow
keys until it passes through the corresponding vertex. The point where these three lines
intersect is the projection point. Although you can't actually trace a line that has been drawn
rather than graphed, you can move the free cursor around using the right and left arrow keys
until it appears to be on the point of intersection.

Enter the x-coordinates of a pair of corresponding vertices into L1 and the y-coordinates into
L2. Use LinReg ([STAT] CALC [4] on the TI-83, and [2nd] [STAT] CALC [5] on the TI-73)
to find the equation of the line. Do this for each pair of corresponding vertices and store each
equation into a different function in Y=. A shortcut for copying the equation into Y= is to
place your cursor in an empty Y= function where you want to put the equation, and press
[VARS] Statistics EQ RegEQ ([2nd] [VARS] Statistics EQ RegEQ on the TI-73).

Now you're ready to graph and draw everything—the three lines and the two triangles. Be
sure all three equations in Y= are highlighted. Recall the picture of the triangles you drew
earlier. Do this by going to the DRAW menu and choosing STO RecallPic, followed by the
number under which you selected to
store the picture. When you press
[ENTER], the equations selected in Y=
will graph. Then your picture will
appear superimposed on the lines.

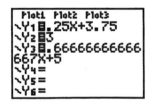

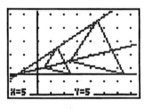

More Than Graphs, Revised Edition • ©2004 Key Curriculum Press

Find the point of intersection of the lines you found earlier. Because the lines are now actually graphed equations, you can use TRACE, or, if you prefer, use the TABLE function and find the x-value whose corresponding y-value is the same for all three functions. The point of intersection of the three lines will be the point of projection. For this sample problem, it is $(-3, 3)$.

Practice Problems

Follow the steps in the activity to find the point of projection for each pair of polygons, using the recommended window.

1. Triangle 1   Triangle 2
   $A_1 = (2, 7)$ $A_2 = (7, 8)$
   $B_1 = (5, 4)$ $B_2 = (13, 2)$
   $C_1 = (4, 9)$ $C_2 = (11, 12)$
   WINDOW: $[-4, 14.8, 2, 0, 12.4, 2, 1]$

2. Triangle 1   Triangle 2
   $A_1 = (4, 21)$ $A_2 = (6, 26)$
   $B_1 = (4, 45)$ $B_2 = (6, 38)$
   $C_1 = (14, 21)$ $C_2 = (11, 26)$
   WINDOW: $[0, 18.8, 2, 20, 51, 4, 1]$

3. Square 1   Square 2
   $A_1 = (20, 20)$ $A_2 = (35, 25)$
   $B_1 = (10, 20)$ $B_2 = (15, 25)$
   $C_1 = (10, 10)$ $C_2 = (15, 5)$
   $D_1 = (21, 10)$ $D_2 = (35, 5)$
   WINDOW: $[0, 47, 5, 0, 31, 5, 1]$

4. Rectangle 1   Rectangle 2
   $A_1 = (11, 18)$ $A_2 = (24, 16)$
   $B_1 = (19, 18)$ $B_2 = (28, 16)$
   $C_1 = (19, 12)$ $C_2 = (28, 13)$
   $D_1 = (11, 12)$ $D_2 = (24, 13)$
   WINDOW: $[10, 33.5, 2, 10, 25.5, 2, 1]$

Extension Problems (TI-82 and TI-83 Only)

Girard Desargues, 1591–1661, was another mathematician who studied projective geometry. He stated a basic theorem that we now call Desargues's theorem. If two triangles have a point of projection, the points of intersection of each pair of corresponding sides will lie on the same line.

Triangles *ABC* and *A'B'C'* are projected from a point *O*. That means that *O* is the point of projection for the two triangles. The coordinates of the triangles' vertices are:

A	(15, 13)	*A'*	(7, 9)
B	(13, 6)	*B'*	(2, 17)
C	(11, 10)	*C'*	(1, 10)

1. Sketch the triangles on a piece of graph paper or draw the triangles on your calculator screen. The WINDOW [0, 18.8, 1, 0, 31, 3, 1] works well for drawing the triangles if you want to use the DRAW screen.
   a. Find the coordinates of point *O*. Enter the equations of the lines of projection in Y1, Y2, and Y3.
   b. Use linear regression to find equations for the lines *AB* and *A'B'*, and store them in Y4 and Y5. You can find the point of intersection of the lines by pressing [2nd] [CALC] and selecting "intersect." You can store these coordinates in L1 and L2. Press [STAT] EDIT and position the cursor where you want the *x*-coordinate to be stored (L1(1)). Press the [X,T,θ,n] key. Now put your cursor on L2(1) and press [ALPHA] [Y] to store the *y*-coordinate. If you store the coordinates this way, the accuracy of the coordinates is maintained.
   c. Find equations for the lines *AC* and *A'C'*, and enter them in Y6 and Y7. Find the point of intersection of the lines. Store the coordinates of this point in L1(2) and L2(2).
   d. Find equations for the lines *BC* and *B'C'*, and enter them in Y8 and Y9. Find the point of intersection of the lines.
   e. Use linear regression to find the equation of the line passing through the points from parts b and c, and enter it in Y0. Check to see if this line also passes through the point you found in part d.
   f. Turn on all of the equations and press [GRAPH] to see Desargues's theorem played out before your eyes!
2. Use one of the practice problems to investigate Desargues's theorem for similar triangles. Where do the lines formed by the corresponding sides seem to intersect?

Projector

Objective: To use linear regression to assist in locating projection points for similar polygons

Materials needed: TI-73, TI-82, TI-83, or TI-83 Plus graphing calculator, graph paper. Extension Problems for TI-82 and TI-83 only.

Appropriate level: Algebra and pre-algebra

Time involved: One hour or class period

Preparation: None

In this activity, students connect algebra and geometry. First they draw a pair of similar polygons on the calculator screen. Then they use the calculator to find the equations of two lines that pass through two pairs of corresponding vertices. The point of intersection of these two lines is the point of projection for the two polygons. The point of intersection can be found using the TRACE function or TABLE function. The diagrams are not necessary, but

I found that the visuals considerably enhance the understanding of what's happening. Most geometry exercises at the middle-school level seldom venture outside the world of planes to study any other geometry besides that of the ancient Greeks. This is a nice excursion that could be used as a starting point for a discussion of visual perspectives that we all experience when we watch something travel toward the horizon.

Solutions

Practice Problems

1. (−3, 6)

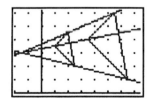

2. (8, 31)

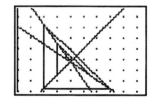

3. (5, 15)

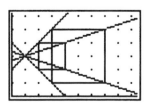

4. (37, 14)

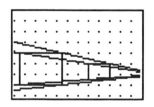

Note on Problem 4: Even though the point of intersection is off the screen, you can still find it by using the TABLE function. You can also trace one of the lines on the graph and find the intersection point. However, if you do this, the entire picture will redraw itself, and the WINDOW values will change. If you recall your original drawing, which is stored, you must first re-input the WINDOW values. You can also save the equations and the WINDOW settings in a Graph Database (StoreGDB). If your window has been changed, you must recall the stored database before recalling the stored picture.

Extension Problems

1. a. (9, 10)

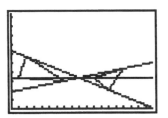

The screens below show the equations for the following lines.

Y1 = AA'	Y4 = B'A'	Y7 = CA
Y2 = BB'	Y5 = BA	Y8 = B'C'
Y3 = CC'	Y6 = C'A'	Y9 = BC

b. The point of intersection of AB and A'B' is (11, 71, 1.47).

c. The point of intersection of AC and A'C' is (9.18, 8.63).

d. The point of intersection of BC and B'C' is (3.2, 25.5).

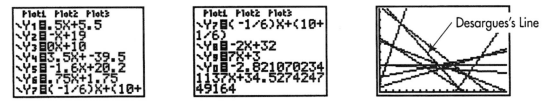

e. The equation Y0 is the equation of the line containing these three points.

2. Answers will vary.

Lake Pepperidge Farm®

Using Sample Data to Make Predictions

Setting the Stage

Part of the job of game wardens and wildlife managers is to be able to make an accurate estimate of the population of certain species within a defined area. One of the most common ways that this is done is through tag-and-release. If an animal population is being studied, the wardens catch a group of the animals and tag them. The animals are then released back into the wild. Later a new group of animals is caught or observed, and the tagged animals are counted. This gives the wardens valuable information on game stocks, migration, and predation. In this activity, you will use tag-and-release to make an estimate of the population of goldfish in Lake Pepperidge Farm.

The Activity

Your task is to make a reasonable prediction of the number of goldfish in a large mixing bowl. By releasing a fixed number of tagged fish, say 200, into the mixing bowl, we will try to make an accurate estimate about the total fish population from a number of samples.

Procedure

Scientists are always careful not to spread disease to a population with which they are working! Be sure you wash your hands before handling the fish.

The mixing bowl should already be almost full of cheddar fish. These will be the untagged fish. Count out 200 of the Parmesan fish. Notice that these are much lighter in color than the cheddar fish and easily identifiable. They will be the tagged fish in this activity. Release these fish into the lake and allow the sample population to integrate. (Mix them.)

If a few fish are spilled, remove them from the experiment. This could simulate *migration*. If you and your classmates would like to sample a few of the crackers, go ahead. This is called *predation* and you have identified yourselves as *predators*.

After the bowl has been well-stirred, you should close your eyes and remove a paper cup full of fish from the lake. This is called *sampling*.

Pour the contents of the cup onto a clean sheet of paper on your desk and count the number of Parmesan fish and cheddar fish in the sample. Record your results.

Tagged fish in *your* sample _____   Untagged fish in *your* sample _____

Now collect the data from all of the samples counted in your class. Record this data in the table.

Number of Tagged Fish (L1)	Number of Untagged Fish (L2)

Total of all samples from your class:

Tagged fish _____ Untagged fish _____

Practice Problems

Enter the number of tagged fish in L1 and the number of untagged fish in L2. Place the cursor at the top of L3 and enter L1/L2. The values in L3 will give you the average ratio of the number of tagged fish to untagged fish for each sample.

1. How similar are these ratios for the different game wardens in your class?
2. Explain why these ratios would be similar or dissimilar.
3. Compute the average of the ratios in L3. To do this, press [STAT] CALC ([2nd] [STAT] CALC on the TI-73). Select 1–Var Stats. Press [2nd] [L3] ([2nd] [STAT] [3] on the TI-73). What is the average of the ratios?
4. Is the average ratio close to your own ratio?
5. Find the ratio of the total number of tagged fish to untagged fish. How close is it to the average ratio for the samples?
6. You can use this information to make an estimate of the total number of fish in the lake. These two ratios will be equal:

$$\frac{\text{number of tagged fish in the lake}}{\text{total number of fish in the lake}} = \frac{\text{number of tagged fish in the sample}}{\text{total number of fish in the sample}}$$

Use this proportion to estimate the total number of fish in Lake Pepperidge Farm. Your estimate of the total fish in the lake _____

7. Why should you get your sample with your eyes closed?
8. How accurate do you think your estimate is? What factors might affect the accuracy of the results?

Extension Problems

1. Do some research and find out what game wardens or wildlife managers in your area do to estimate a population.
2. Do some research about one of your favorite wild animals, birds, or fish. Find out how studies have been done to estimate their populations in a certain region.

TEACHER NOTES

Lake Pepperidge Farm®

Objective: To use a data sample to make a prediction about an entire population
Materials needed: TI-73, TI-82, TI-83, or TI-83 Plus graphing calculator, very large mixing bowl, small paper cups, jumbo package of Pepperidge Farm® Goldfish (cheddar), small package of Pepperidge Farm® Goldfish (Parmesan)
Appropriate level: Algebra and pre-algebra
Time involved: One hour or class period
Preparation: Experience with finding the unknown in a proportion

In certain parts of the country, close attention is being paid to the reduced sizes of the salmon runs. Seasons are shortened by fishery officials, and many commercial fishermen are challenging the claim that there is any real justification for this. This lesson fits in very well with reports in the media. Obviously, game wardens cannot just don scuba gear and go down and count the fish. Some of the students who have caught tagged fish also pointed out that the state provides a reward for reporting these fish as a tool to improve the accuracy of their fish counts. This activity turned out to be both timely and a lot of fun.

Decide whether to have your students work in pairs, teams, or alone, depending on how many students you have and how many fish there are. This activity works well with pairs. That way you will have a larger number of samples than you would with the class divided into groups. Ask each pair or group to record their data on the chalkboard, a transparency, or a large piece of paper. Then have each student record this data in the table provided in the activity. If students need more lines on which to enter data, they can construct a table similar to the one shown.

Solutions

Practice Problems

Answers will vary.

Extension Problems

Answers will vary.

Life Span
Evaluating Data and Drawing Conclusions About Life Expectancy

Setting the Stage

"Never send to know for whom the bell tolls; it tolls for thee."

—John Donne

Insurance agents know that the premium or cost of an insurance policy is based on the likelihood of a claim being filed. In the case of life insurance, the insurance company is making a bet that the client will survive. The client is betting that he or she will not, in which case a cash value will be forwarded to his or her beneficiary. The fairness of the amount of the premium and the value of the policy are all based on mathematical statistics gathered from large samples of individuals in what is called a **mortality table**. One of the earliest mortality tables was compiled by Edmund Halley, for whom the comet is named, in 1693. The data in mortality tables is used to make predictions about the life spans of people who are still alive.

The Activity

To make accurate predictions, you need to collect a large amount of data that is unbiased. By collecting data from the obituaries in a newspaper at times other than a natural disaster, you can make a reasonable estimate of the life spans of the citizens in your community. Larger samples gathered from a larger area will increase the credibility of your conclusions.

Collect at least 20 obituary notices from local newspapers. Enter the ages of the people as data lists using L1 for females and L2 for males.

Now press [STAT] CALC [1] ([2nd] [STAT] CALC [1] on the TI-73). The calculator will display 1–Var Stats. Press [2nd] [L1] ([2nd] [STAT] [1] on the TI-73) to specify L1, and press [ENTER].

The calculator display should look something like this:

In this example, $\bar{x}$ is the average of all the entries in L1, $\sum x$ is the sum of all the entries in L1, and n indicates the number of entries in L1.

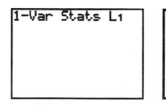

```
1-Var Stats L1
```

```
1-Var Stats
x̄=65.93
Σx=1780.00
Σx²=127324.08
Sx=19.59
σx=19.22
↓n=27.00
```

The other values concern the sum of the squares, and standard deviations, which you won't be using in this activity.

Press the down cursor repeatedly, to see more information about the sample.

In this window, you can see the smallest value in the list, the values at each quartile, the median, and the maximum.

Use the calculator to fill in the chart for your mortality data.

	Females	Males
n		
$\bar{x}$		
min		
Q_1		
med		
Q_3		
max		

Practice Problems

1. Why would a newspaper from Tampa, Florida, or Lake Havasu, Arizona, be a poor resource for this data?
2. Would collecting all the data gathered by the class into a large pool enhance or diminish the quality of the data? Explain your answer.
3. Using your own data as a predictor, to what age do you have a 75% chance of survival? a 50% chance? a 25% chance?
4. Can this data be used to predict the precise life span of any certain individual?

Extension Problems

1. You can also display the obituary data very effectively in a box plot. Press [2nd] [STAT PLOT] ([2nd] [PLOT] on the TI-73) and choose Plot1. Set it up as a box plot of L1, with frequency 1. If you graph the data from L1 in Plot1 and the data from L2 in Plot2 on the same screen, you can visually compare the life spans for males and females. Do this, and write a paragraph explaining any similarities and differences you notice in the graphs.

2. In an almanac you can find data about life expectancy. Do some research and compare the life-expectancy numbers in an almanac to your results. How close are they? What other factors does the data in the almanac take into consideration?

3. Collect data from an almanac related to life expectancy. Make some graphs and prepare a short report related to what you learned. Present the report to the class.

Life Span

<table>
<tr><td align="right">Objective:</td><td>To evaluate data and draw conclusions about human life span</td></tr>
<tr><td align="right">Materials needed:</td><td>TI-73, TI-82, TI-83, or TI-83 Plus graphing calculator, newspapers (You may want to start collecting these several weeks before you do this activity.)</td></tr>
<tr><td align="right">Appropriate level:</td><td>Algebra and pre-algebra</td></tr>
<tr><td align="right">Time involved:</td><td>One hour or class period</td></tr>
<tr><td align="right">Preparation:</td><td>Familiarity with STAT functions on the TI-73, TI-82, TI-83, or TI-83 Plus</td></tr>
</table>

My students have told me that they enjoy lessons more when they are based on real, observable data. Real math involves real data. It's especially impressive when all the data comes from several different sources and still corroborates the same conclusion. I ask the student teams to collect individual data sets from independent sources, and then post them all in the front of the room. We base our calculations on the combined set of data rather than trying to draw an individual conclusion from each sample set. A word of caution—you will need to be sure the combined set of data does not have overlaps. According to the Law of Large Numbers, this should enhance the accuracy of our conclusions.

Students think a lot about their own mortality, even if they don't talk about it much. They paid very close attention. The boys in the class thought that it was unfair that female life spans tend to be longer than male life spans. It was hard for them to understand that "fairness" to an individual is not an attribute of death. It is important for students to realize that this data defines trends only for large populations and cannot be used fairly to predict the life span of any specific individual.

We had some good discussions with this lesson. Most samples had the obituary of at least one teenager. They found this very interesting and pointed out that the teenager in the article could have been very similar to themselves. A useful point to notice is that longevity seems to be an inherent factor in some families, and none of us can control who our parents are. Even though longevity can be scientifically explained through genetics, the students still seem to feel that it's not right, or at least not fair.

Solutions

Practice Problems

1. Answers will vary. Places like Lake Havasu, Arizona, and Tampa, Florida, tend to have a much older population, which would tend to skew the data.
2. Answers will vary. A larger sample would improve the data; however, if there is overlap in the data, then this would diminish its validity.
3. Answers will vary.
4. No, the data cannot be used to predict the precise life span of an individual person.

Extension Problems

Answers will vary.

Circle Graphs

Displaying Data in a Circle Graph Format

Setting the Stage

A circle graph is a quick way to get an accurate picture of the distribution of an entire population. The circle represents the total of all possible outcomes in what looks like a pie. The size of each piece of the pie corresponds to the number of people or responses that it represents. Although circle graphs are not among the TI-82's and TI-83's library of functions, there is a program at the end of this activity that will allow you to create a circle graph on the calculator. This utility resides in the plotter on the TI-73 and does not require a program.

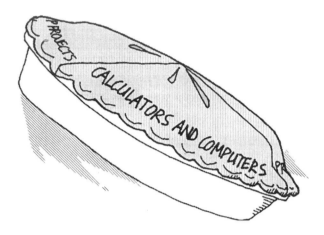

The Activity

Imagine that you have polled your classmates on the question "What do you like best about math?" You offered them the choices shown in the table below where you have tallied their responses.

Which activities did you like best in math class this year?	Responses	Total
Graphing	✓✓✓	3
Problem solving	✓✓✓✓	4
Calculators and computers	✓✓✓✓✓✓✓✓	8
Group projects	✓✓✓✓✓	5
Compasses and construction of models	✓	1

Using the TI-82 and TI-83

If you are using a TI-82 or TI-83, enter the program found on the following page.

Before running the program, enter the data in L1. In this case, L1 = {3, 4, 8, 5, 1}. You can use this data and the program to create a circle graph of the data. Run the program CIRCGRPH. The program will ask you if you want to display the data or percentages.

More Than Graphs, Revised Edition • ©2004 Key Curriculum Press

If you choose 2:PERCENTAGES, the calculator will convert the data to percentages. In this case 14.3% of the people asked chose option 1, graphing. If you choose 2:DATA, it will display the raw data you collected in a circle graph.

From the circle graph, you can see that the most popular choice was option 3, calculators and computers. This was chosen by 38.1% of the class.

Opening Screen for CIRCGRPH

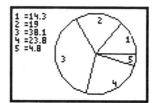

TI-82/TI-83 Pie Chart

PROGRAM:CIRCGRPH
Param:Degree
AxesOff:PlotsOff :FnOff
1-Var Stats L1
"3cos(T)"→X1T
"3sin(T)"→Y1T
0→Tmin:360→Tmax:5→Tstep
⁻6→Xmin:3.4→Xmax:1→Xscl
⁻3.1→Ymin:3.1→Ymax:1→Yscl
Menu("DATA DISPLAYED?","PERCENTAGES",1,"DATA",2)
Lbl 1:0→F:Goto 3
Lbl 2:1→F
Lbl 3
0→A:sum(L1)→P
For(C,1,n)
360L1(C)/P→B
A+B→A
Line(0,0,X1T(A),Y1T(A))
Text(28-int(25*sin(A-.5B)+.5),60+int(25cos(A-.5B)+.5),C)
If C≤10:Then
Text(6(C−1),0,C)
Text(6(C−1),7,"=")
L1(C)→X
If F=0:100round(X/P,3)→X
Text(6(C−1),11,X)
End
End

Using the TI-73

For the sample question, create two lists, named LIKES and TOTAL. (Column titles must always be from one to five characters in length.) Do this by going to the LIST screen and moving left until the cursor reaches a blank column. Use [2nd] [TEXT] to enter the characters.

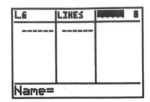 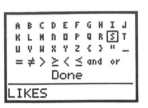 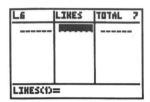

Then enter abbreviated titles, using the TEXT editor for the categories under LIKES and the values 3, 4, 8, 5, and 1 under TOTAL. *Characters that will not be used as variables must be bracketed in quotes.* The quotation marks will not count as one of the five characters.

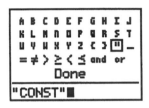 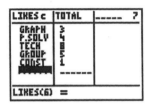

Set up the plot by going to the plotter ([2nd] [PLOT]). Use the cursor to select the pie chart icon. Use [2nd] [STAT] and the cursor to choose the LIKES and TOTAL categories for CategList and DataList. Use the [GRAPH] key to see the pie chart.

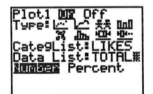 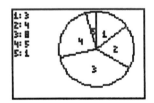

Plotter Screen   TI-73 Pie Chart

Practice Problems

1. The data in the table gives the populations of major world areas for 1998 and the projected populations for 2050. Use the CIRCGRPH program or the calculator's pie chart feature on the TI-73 to make a circle graph that pictures the data. Record the percentages for each graph. Write a sentence or two describing any trends you notice in these two graphs.

Area	1998 Population (in millions)	Percentage	2050 Population (in millions)	Percentage
Europe	508		486	
North America	301		326	
Oceania	30		41	
USSR*	291		380	
Africa	761		2,265	
Latin America	508		992	
China	1,237		1,521	
India	984		1,699	
Other Asia	1,307		2,379	

*Republics of former Soviet Union, *The Universal Almanac 1999*

2. Create a question of your own and collect responses from your classmates. Enter the responses in L1, and use the CIRCGRPH program to display the data. Make a printout if possible.

Extension Problem

Look in your local want ads at the salaries offered for jobs that are advertised. Check also for housing costs and ask around about other expenses involved in living in a house or apartment. Enter the various living expenses in L1, and use the CIRCGRPH program or the calculator's pie chart feature on the TI-73 to generate a circle graph of your budget. Don't forget to budget for savings, entertainment, and food. What is the total amount you would spend each month? Would you be able to afford this based on the salaries listed in the paper?

Circle Graphs

Objective:	To display data in a circle graph format
Materials needed:	TI-73, TI-82, TI-83, or TI-83 Plus graphing calculator
Appropriate level:	Algebra and pre-algebra
Time involved:	One hour or one class period
Preparation:	Experience with computing percentages

Some students may have difficulty entering the program in this activity because it involves a number of commands that may be difficult for them to find quickly. For this reason you may want to encourage students to transfer the program by linking.

Conducting a survey and tallying the responses makes this activity much more meaningful. Students enjoy choosing their questions and are very enthusiastic in soliciting responses.

Care should be taken, however, in making sure students understand how to generate good surveys. The responses need to be mutually exclusive if students are going to display their results in a circle graph.

I had students print out their circle graphs using the TI-GRAPH LINK™ and a computer. Coloring each section of the graph added clarity to the circle graphs. Students found this program helpful for other classes as well.

Solutions

Practice Problems

1.

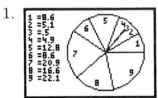 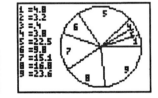

2. Answers will vary.

Extension Problem

Answers will vary.

The Chaos Game

Exploring Chaos with a Fractal Pattern

Setting the Stage

A relatively new scientific endeavor is the theory of chaos—how the slightest change in a physical system can cause wildly different results. A simple example is the difficulty meteorologists have in making accurate weather predictions. Sometimes very small, almost imperceptible, changes can create very different conditions, thus making it very difficult to make accurate predictions. Conversely, you might be surprised to find order, or a pattern, out of seemingly random, chaotic events. The sometimes beautiful and exotic patterns that do result from chaos are called *fractals*.

The Activity

The game of Chaos uses a pencil and ruler; a spinner with three equal sections labeled 0, 1, and 2; and a piece of paper on which you draw an equilateral triangle with the corners labeled 0, 1, and 2. To get your starting point, close your eyes and put a point somewhere on the paper.

Now begin to move by spinning the spinner. If it lands on a 2, then use your ruler to mark a point halfway between the corner labeled 2 and the starting point. Similarly, if the spinner lands on 0 or 1, move halfway from the last point you drew to the corresponding corner. Then spin again and move halfway from this new point to the corner dictated by your spin. Instead of a spinner, you could use a regular die. Move to corner 1 on a roll of 1 or 4, to corner 2 if the roll is 2 or 5, and to corner 0 when you roll a 3 or 6. To understand how the game is played, try it and locate at least 20 points. Do you see a pattern emerging? What do you think will happen after many such points are located?

Because the choice of which corner to move to is random, you might expect the result to be a triangle full of dots. To see the pattern that emerges, you will probably have to put 500 to 1000 dots on the paper! Rather than plot each of these points by hand, you can use this program that plays the game for you, just a little faster.

TI-82/TI-83 Program

```
PROGRAM:CHAOS
ClrDraw
While not(getKey)
Pt-On(X,Y)
int(3rand)→T
(X+T)/2→X
(Y+(T=1))/2→Y
End
```

TI-73 Program

```
PROGRAM:CHAOS
ClrDraw:PlotsOff
Input "NUMBER OF POINTS",P
For(L,1,P,1)
Pt-On(X,Y)
int(3rand)→T
(X+T)/2→X
(Y+(T=1))/2→Y
End
Pause
```

This program does not set the windows for you. Before running it, be sure you are in Function mode, and turn all functions and stat plots off. Set the window for 0 to 2 on the x-axis and 0 to 1 on the y-axis. Set both Xscl and Yscl to 0.

Practice Problems

1. The result when you run this program is a pattern of dots that appears anything but haphazard. The pattern is a fractal called Sierpiński's triangle. You can pause the program by pressing any key except the ON key. Pressing CLEAR ENTER will restart the program from where it left off. If you want to start the plot over, you will have to clear the screen by pressing 2nd [DRAW] 1 (DRAW 1 on the TI-73) before running the program again.

    To show the "self-similarity" of this fractal, zoom in on any of the smaller triangles in the picture and run the program again. For example, change Xmin to 1 and Ymax to 0.5 to zoom in on the lower right triangle. The same Sierpiński's triangle appears, but it takes four times longer because the program is plotting points in the entire triangle and the window is looking at only one-quarter of it. Describe what you see.

2. Run the game ten times with different windows. Describe any patterns that emerge.

Extension Problem

Do some research and find out how fractals or chaos theory is being applied to a real-world problem. Prepare a short report that you can give to the class.

The Chaos Game

Objective:	To use the calculator to investigate chaos and fractals
Materials needed:	TI-73, TI-82, TI-83, or TI-83 Plus graphing calculator
Appropriate level:	Algebra and pre-algebra
Time involved:	One hour or class period
Preparation:	None

This activity explores the idea that patterns can emerge from chaos. Encourage students to actually plot points using the rules given before running the program so they will understand how the points are generated. This is a somewhat difficult program for most students to understand, but a detailed explanation is given below. You may or may not want to share this with your students.

A few programming notes: The first and last lines of the program set up a loop that keeps the program plotting points until a key is pressed. "While" and "getKey" can be found in the CTL and I/O submenus, respectively, of the PROGRAM menu.

The command **Pt-On (X,Y)** plots a point at the new coordinate (x, y) that is computed in the next three lines. Note that the first point plotted is "random" in the sense that it is the last (x, y) value used in whatever graph you were doing previously.

The command **int 3rand → T** picks a random number 0, 1, or 2, and stores it temporarily in T. Look at the following table:

T	Move to Corner #	Coordinates of the Corner
0	0	$(0, 0)$
1	1	$(1, 1)$
2	2	$(2, 0)$

Note that the x-coordinate, in each case, matches the roll, T, so the new x-coordinate is halfway between the current one, x, and the new one, T. Therefore, the average of x and T gives the new coordinate. Thus, $(X + T)/2$ is stored in X.

The y-coordinate is just a little harder to compute. Basically, we want the new y-coordinate to be 0 unless $T = 1$. The code $(T = 1)$, though strange, accomplishes this task. In short it asks, "Does $T = 1$?" A "yes" response is converted in the calculator to a 1, and a "no" is represented by 0. Thus, $(T = 1)$ evaluates to 1 when T is 1, and otherwise it equals 0. Thus, $(Y + (T = 1))/2$ averages the y-value and 1 when $T = 1$, and it averages the y-value and 0 when the roll, T, is either 0 or 2. It does exactly what we want it to do.

A slightly more sophisticated version of the program appears on the next page. This version will automatically set the windows. This program will automatically count the dots as they are being plotted. However, you will not be able to start and stop the plot as you could with the original version.

TI-82/TI-83 Program

```
PROGRAM:CHAOS2
ClrDraw:0→N
FnOff :PlotsOff
0→Xmin:2→Xmax:0→Xscl
0→Ymin:1→Ymax:0→Yscl
While not(getKey)
Pt-On(X,Y)
int(3rand)→T
(X+T)/2→X
(Y+(T=1))/2→Y
N+1→N
Text(5,5,N)
End
```

TI-73 Program

```
PROGRAM:CHAOS2
ClrDraw:0→N
FnOff :PlotsOff
0→Xmin:2→Xmax:0→Xscl
0→Ymin:1→Ymax:0→Yscl
Input "NUMBER OF POINTS",P
For(L,1,P,1)
Pt-On(X,Y)
int(3rand)→T
(X+T)/2→X
(Y+(T=1))/2→Y
N+1→N
Text(5,5,N)
End::0→N
FnOff :PlotsOff
0→Xmin:2→Xmax:0→Xscl
0→Ymin:1→Ymax:0→Yscl
Pause
```

Solutions

Practice Problems

Answers will vary.

Extension Problem

Answers will vary.

Close Contact: A Simulation for Modern Times

STAT PROG

Simulating a Viral Transmission

Setting the Stage

Many viruses are transmitted among human populations. Chicken pox, hepatitis A, the common cold, and the Ebola virus are examples of viruses. Some viruses, like chicken pox, are transmitted through the air (they are *airborne*). If a person infected with an airborne virus sneezes or coughs in your general vicinity, you may become infected. Other viruses are transmitted through contact with mucous membranes. If you, for example, drink from a glass used by a person infected with a virus of this kind, you may introduce the virus into your system.

In this activity, you will model a virus that is running rampant in your community of calculators. Any calculator your calculator comes in contact with may be carrying the virus even though there are no symptoms. This models the fact that for many viruses, victims are often most contagious in the 24-hour period before they become sick. This particular disease is fatal so you will have to keep checking to see if your calculator is still alive.

After doing the simulation, you will use mathematics to assist you in your study of the disease and help you understand the impact the virus may have on the population.

The Activity

Enter the three programs in your calculator. CONINIT initializes your calculator, CONTACT determines the status (alive or dead) of your calculator during the simulation, and CONDIAG determines whether your calculator is a carrier of the virus at the end of the simulation.

TI-82/TI-83 Programs

```
PROGRAM:CONINIT
ClrHome
0→A
0→L
Disp "SURVIVABILITY"
Input S
PROGRAM:CONTACT
ClrHome
rand→X
max(A,L)→L
max(A,L)→A
X*L→X
If X>S
Then
Disp "SORRY,YOUR","TI DIED."
Else
Disp "GOOD,YOUR
TI","SURVIVED."
Disp "CONTINUE PLAY"
PROGRAM:CONDIAG
ClrHome
If L=1
Then
Disp "YOUR TI CARRIES","THE
INFECTION."
Else
Disp "YOUR TI IS
NOT","INFECTED."
```

TI-73 Program

```
PROGRAM:CONINIT
ClrScreen
0→A
0→L
Disp "SURVIVABILITY"
Input S
PROGRAM:CONTACT
ClrScreen
rand→X
max(A,L)→L
max(A,L)→A
X*L→X
If X>S
Then
Disp "SORRY,YOUR","TI DIED."
Pause
Else
Disp "GOOD,YOUR
TI","SURVIVED."
Disp "CONTINUE PLAY"
Pause
PROGRAM:CONDIAG
ClrScreen
If L=1
Then
Disp "YOUR TI CARRIES","THE
INFECTION."
Pause
Else
Disp "YOUR TI IS
NOT","INFECTED."
Pause
```

To begin the game, run the CONINIT program. Input 0.6 as the SURVIVABILITY rate. Mark your calculator so you can identify it. Your teacher will collect all of the calculators and "infect" one or two of them with the virus. When the calculators are returned, the simulation can begin.

Link your calculator with someone else's to model being exposed to the virus. Decide who will transmit and who will receive. The transmitter will send the variable A to the receiver. To do this, the receiver presses [2nd] [LINK] RECEIVE [ENTER]. The transmitter presses [2nd] [LINK], selects All, scrolls down to A, presses [ENTER], scrolls right to TRANSMIT, and presses [ENTER]. (The LINK feature is listed under the [APPS] key on the TI-73.) After the link, the student who received the transmission runs the CONTACT program to see if his or her calculator survived and keeps a tally of the number of nonfatal links.

Continue linking until your calculator dies or the simulation is over. Be sure to interact with as many different calculators as you can. However, you can interact with the same calculator more than once. Try to alternate between being a receiver and a transmitter. Be sure to run CONTACT after each time you receive.

If your calculator is a survivor when the simulation is ended, run the program CONDIAG to see if your calculator is infected with the virus.

If your calculator doesn't survive, record the number of links your calculator had before it succumbed to the virus.

Practice Problems

1. Make a tally of the class results showing the number of links for each nonsurviving calculator.

Links	Frequency
1	
2	
3	
4	
5	
6	
7	
8	
9	
10	

2. Display the data on the grid below, showing appropriate labels for the graph title, axes, and scale.

3. Write a few sentences describing the relationship between the number of links and the chances of being fatally infected with the virus. Is it possible to become a fatality after having only one exposure?
4. What was the total number of survivors at the end of play? _____
   How many of the survivors were carrying the infection? _____
   What percentage of the surviving population was infected? _____
5. Are there some strategies that might have helped slow down the spread of the virus? Write a paragraph summarizing your conclusions from the simulation.

Extension Problems
Changing Parameters

1. Your personal hygiene habits can greatly influence becoming infected by or spreading a virus. Do the simulation again, but this time each student will enter his or her own survivability rate. This rate will be determined by the personal hygiene habits of the individual being studied (your calculator). Each person should choose his or her own survivability rate somewhere between 0.2 and 0.9, depending on the personal hygiene habits of the subject. The higher the number you choose, the better are your chances of survival.
2. Make a scatter plot comparing the survivability rate and the number of exposures each calculator survived. (You can do this by entering the survivability rates in L1 and the corresponding number of links, before the calculator died or when the simulation ended, in L2.) Can you draw any conclusions regarding personal hygiene habits and the likelihood of surviving the outbreak of a virus?

Close Contact: A Simulation for Modern Times

Objective: To simulate a viral transmission

Materials needed: Class set of TI-73, TI-82, TI-83, or TI-83 Plus graphing calculators, writing instruments (Mixing the TI-73s, TI-82s, TI-83s, and TI-83 Pluses may technically work, but it will slow down the exercise greatly and focus the students' attention on button pushing instead of the spread of the virus.)

Appropriate level: Pre-algebra through college

Time involved: One hour or class period for programming and play, another for reflection, graphing, and analysis

Preparation: Experience with linking the graphing calculators

In this activity, students simulate the spread of a virus by linking their calculators and transmitting the value of a variable. A random process determines whether the calculator becomes infected and, if it becomes infected, whether it survives. After the simulation, students share their data and look for relationships between the survivability rate and the number of contacts (links).

Here is how the simulation is run:

1. Be certain that students label their calculators so they know which one is theirs.

2. All students run the CONINIT program. It clears out old data that may interfere with the simulation and allows students to set the survivability rate. The first time the game is played, have each student input a survivability rate of 0.6.

3. Collect all of the calculators in a bag or box. Out of view of the students, assign a value of 1 to the variable A ([1] [STO▶] [ALPHA] A [ENTER] on the TI-82 and TI-83, and [1] [STO▶] [2nd] [TEXT] A [ENTER] on the TI-73) in one or two calculators. Return the calculators to students.

4. For 10 minutes, students will link repeatedly with other students. For each link, one student will transmit and the other student will receive. After the link, the student who received the transmission will run the CONTACT program to see if his or her calculator survived. Once a student's calculator succumbs to the virus, the student will record the number of times he or she received a transmission on a class tally sheet.

5. At the end of 10 minutes, students whose calculators survived will run the CONDIAG program to see if their calculators are infected. Record how many calculators survived and how many of those are infected with the virus.

Solutions

Practice Problems

Answers will vary.

Extension Problems

Changing Parameters

The Extension Problems explore how individual habits can affect the impact of a virus. Students choose a survivability rate within a given range to simulate a range of personal hygiene habits. This can reflect any number of personal choices from eating right and exercising to good handwashing and wise personal choices.

Once students have chosen survivability rates, collect the calculators, infect one or two, and then return them. Repeat the simulation and have students tally their results. When the simulation is complete, help the students to create a scatter plot comparing the survivability rates to the frequency of exposures. Compare results to the data from the first simulation.

This activity should provide a great deal of material for written reflection to be included in student journals or portfolios.

APPENDIX: KEY MAPS

TI-73	TI-82	TI-83
TEXT		
STAT	STAT	STAT
DRAW	DRAW	DRAW
PROG	PROG	PROG
FUNC	FUNC	FUNC
PROB	PROB	PROB
	SEQ	SEQ
	PARA	PARA
	MATRX	MATRX

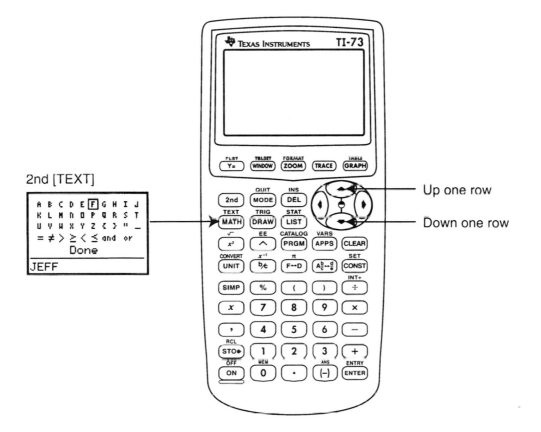

2nd [TEXT]

Up one row

Down one row

STAT

2nd [PLOT]

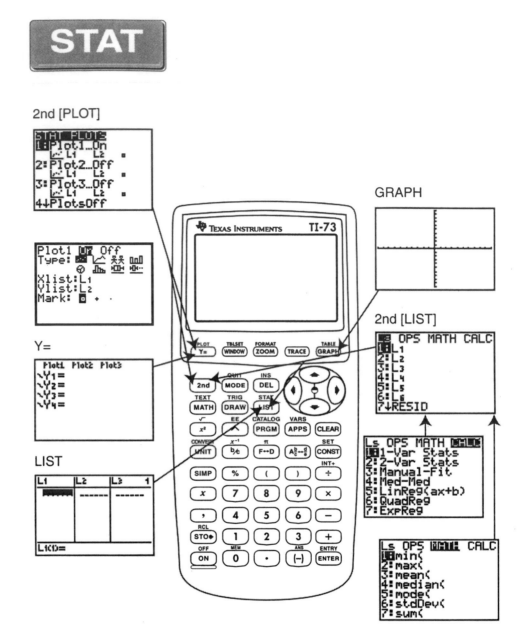

Y=

LIST

GRAPH

2nd [LIST]

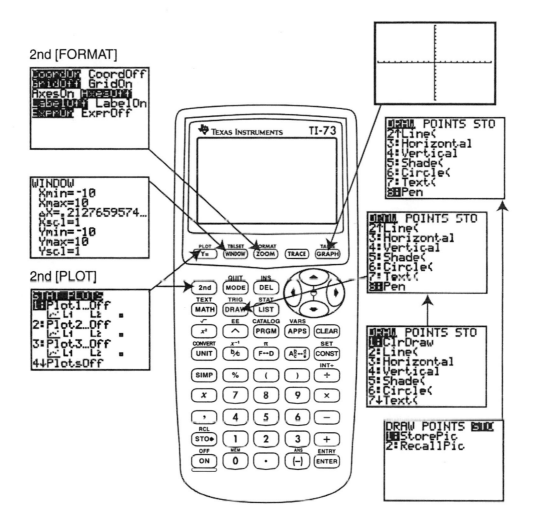

2nd [FORMAT]

```
CoordOn CoordOff
GridOff GridOn
AxesOn AxesOff
LabelOff LabelOn
ExprOn ExprOff
```

```
WINDOW
 Xmin=-10
 Xmax=10
 ΔX=.2127659574...
 Xscl=1
 Ymin=-10
 Ymax=10
 Yscl=1
```

2nd [PLOT]

```
STAT PLOTS
1 Plot1…Off
   ⌐ L₁  L₂   .
2: Plot2…Off
   ⌐ L₁  L₂   .
3: Plot3…Off
   ⌐ L₁  L₂   .
4↓PlotsOff
```

```
DRAW POINTS STO
2↑Line(
3:Horizontal
4:Vertical
5:Shade(
6:Circle(
7:Text(
8 Pen
```

```
DRAW POINTS STO
2↑Line(
3:Horizontal
4:Vertical
5:Shade(
6:Circle(
7:Text(
8 Pen
```

```
DRAW POINTS STO
1 ClrDraw
2:Line(
3:Horizontal
4:Vertical
5:Shade(
6:Circle(
7↓Text(
```

```
DRAW POINTS STO
1 StorePic
2:RecallPic
```

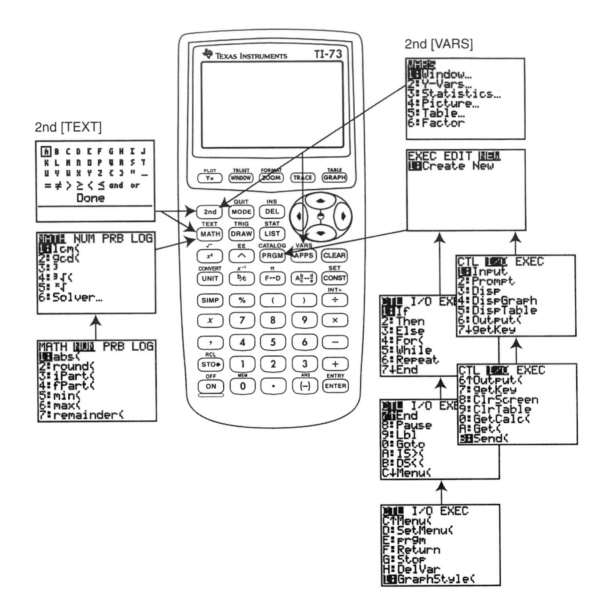

FUNC

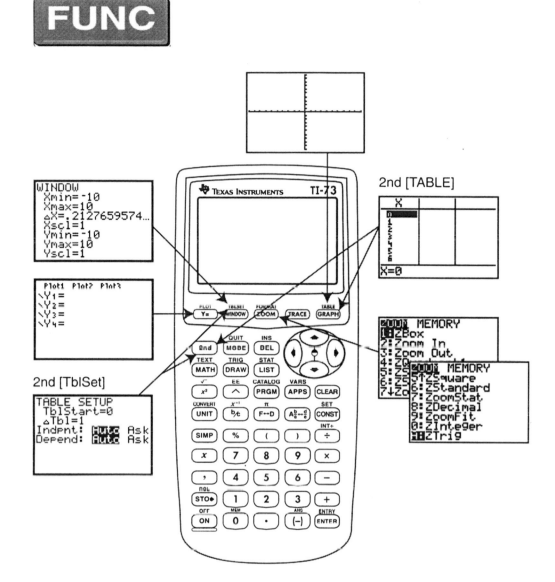

WINDOW
Xmin=-10
Xmax=10
△X=.2127659574…
Xscl=1
Ymin=-10
Ymax=10
Yscl=1

Plot1 Plot2 Plot3
\Y1=
\Y2=
\Y3=
\Y4=

2nd [TblSet]

TABLE SETUP
TblStart=0
△Tbl=1
Indpnt: Auto Ask
Depend: Auto Ask

2nd [TABLE]

X

X=0

ZOOM MEMORY
1:ZBox
2:Zoom In
3:Zoom Out
4:ZD
5:ZS
6:ZS
7↓Zo

ZOOM MEMORY
5:ZSquare
6:ZStandard
7:ZoomStat
8:ZDecimal
9:ZoomFit
0:ZInteger
A:ZTrig

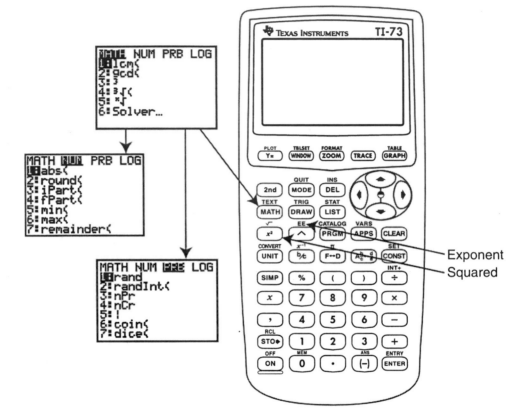

Exponent

Squared

2nd [STAT PLOT]

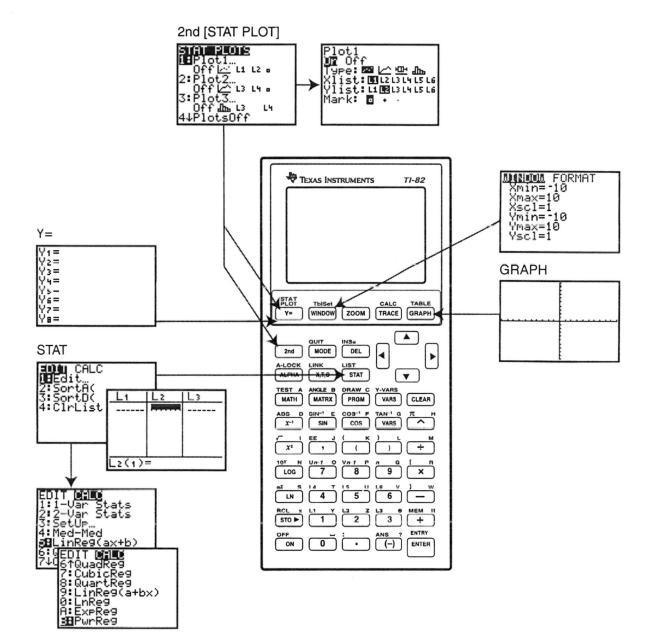

DRAW

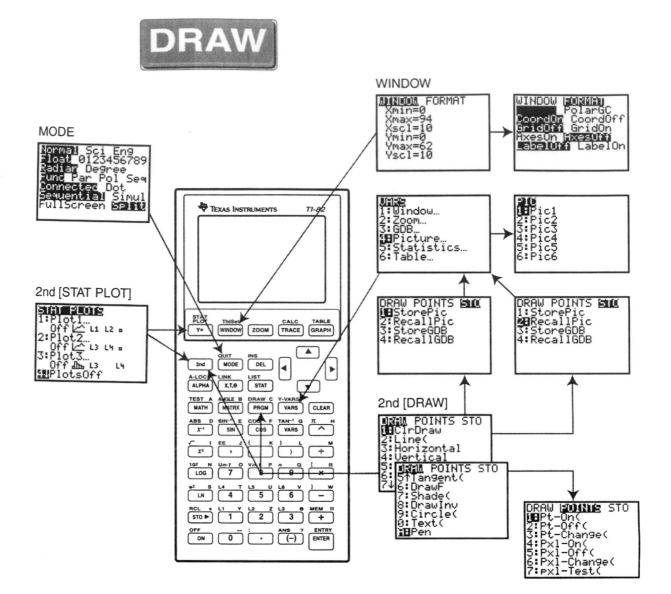

MODE

WINDOW

2nd [STAT PLOT]

2nd [DRAW]

PROG

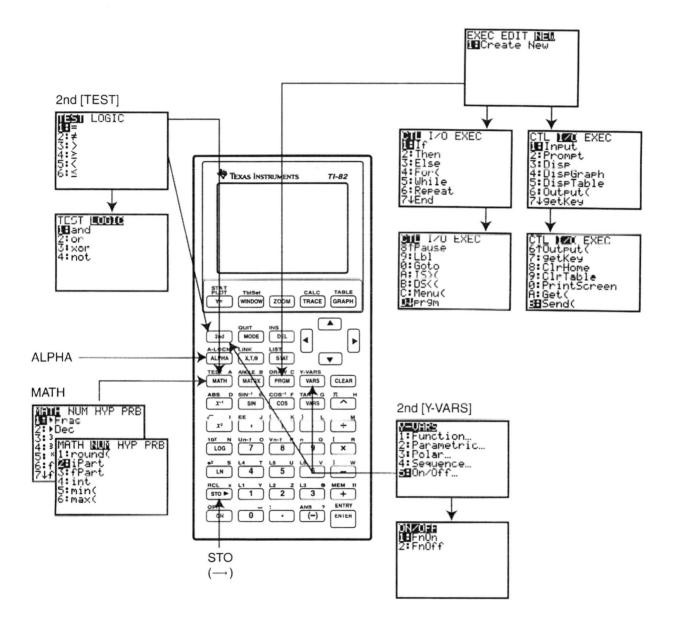

2nd [TEST]

TEST LOGIC
1:=
2:≠
3:>
4:≥
5:<
6:≤

TEST LOGIC
1:and
2:or
3:xor
4:not

EXEC EDIT NEW
1:Create New

CTL I/O EXEC
1:If
2:Then
3:Else
4:For(
5:While
6:Repeat
7↓End

CTL I/O EXEC
1:Input
2:Prompt
3:Disp
4:DispGraph
5:DispTable
6:Output(
7↓getKey

CTL I/O EXEC
8:Pause
9:Lbl
0:Goto
A:IS>(
B:DS<(
C:Menu(
D:prgm

CTL I/O EXEC
6↑Output(
7:getKey
8:ClrHome
9:ClrTable
0:PrintScreen
A:Get(
B:Send(

ALPHA

MATH

MATH NUM HYP PRB
1:▶Frac
2:▶Dec
3:3
4:3√
5:×√
6:f
7↓f

MATH NUM HYP PRB
1:round(
2:iPart
3:fPart
4:int
5:min(
6:max(

2nd [Y-VARS]

Y-VARS
1:Function…
2:Parametric…
3:Polar…
4:Sequence…
5:On/Off…

ON/OFF
1:FnOn
2:FnOff

STO
(→)

FUNC

2nd [TABLE]

X		
0		
1		
2		
3		
4		
5		
6		

X=0

2nd [TblSet]

TABLE SETUP
 TblMin=0
 △Tbl=1
 Indpnt: **Auto** Ask
 Depend: **Auto** Ask

Y=

Y1=
Y2=
Y3=
Y4=
Y5=
Y6=
Y7=
Y8=

WINDOW FORMAT
 Xmin=-10
 Xmax=10
 Xscl=1
 Ymin=-10
 Ymax=10
 Yscl=1

TRACE

GRAPH

ZOOM

ZOOM MEMORY
1:ZBox
2:Zoom In
3: **ZOOM** MEMORY
4: 3:Zoom Out
5: 4:ZDecimal
6: 5:ZSquare
7:↓ 6:ZStandard
 7:ZTrig
 8:ZInteger
 9:ZoomStat

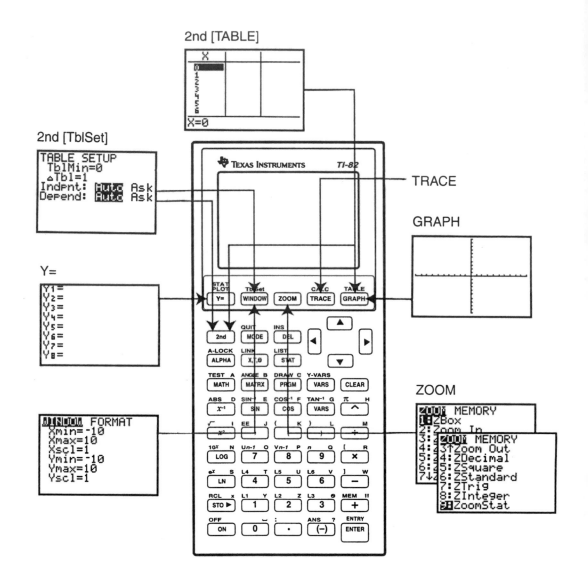

More Than Graphs, Revised Edition • ©2004 Key Curriculum Press

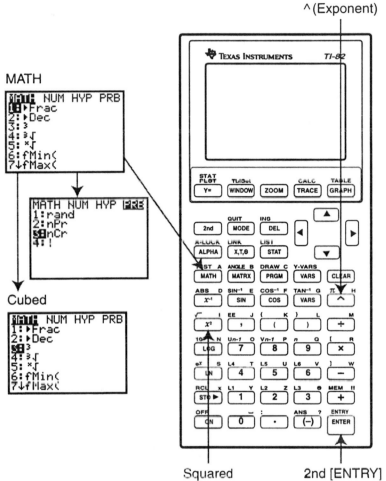

PROB

MATH

```
MATH NUM HYP PRB
1▶Frac
2:▶Dec
3:³
4:³√
5:ˣ√
6:fMin(
7↓fMax(
```

```
MATH NUM HYP PRB
1:rand
2:nPr
3:nCr
4:!
```

Cubed

```
MATH NUM HYP PRB
1:▶Frac
2:▶Dec
3:³
4:³√
5:ˣ√
6:fMin(
7↓fMax(
```

^(Exponent)

Squared   2nd [ENTRY]

WINDOW

```
WINDOW FORMAT
 UnStart=1
 VnStart=.78539…
 nStart=1
 nMin=1
 nMax=20
 Xmin=0
↓Xmax=20
```

```
WINDOW FORMAT
↑nMax=20
 Xmin=0
 Xmax=20
 Xscl=1
 Ymin=.6
 Ymax=.9
 Yscl=.5
```

MODE

```
Normal Sci Eng
Float 0123456789
Radian Degree
Func Par Pol Seq
Connected Dot
Sequential Simul
FullScreen Split
```

Y=

```
Un=Un-1 -((-1)^n/
(2n-1))
Vn=π/4
```

GRAPH

2nd [TblSet]

```
TABLE SETUP
 TblMin=1
 ∆Tbl=1
 Indpnt: Auto Ask
 Depend: Auto Ask
```

2nd [π]

2nd [Un-1]

2nd [n]

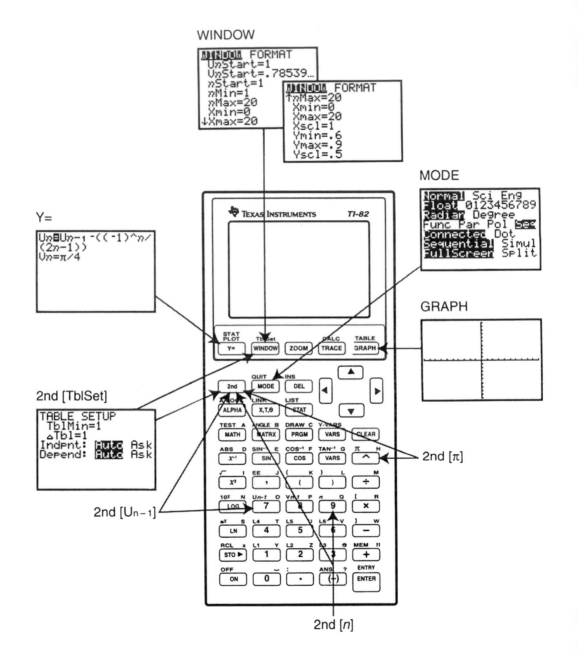

PARA

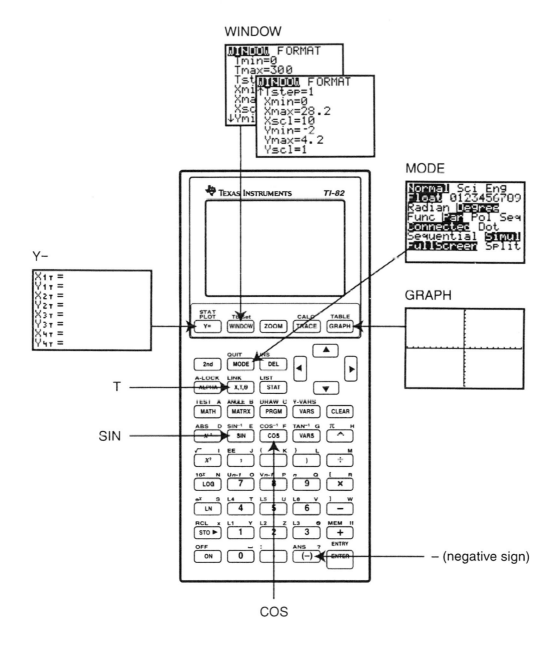

WINDOW

```
WINDOW FORMAT
 Tmin=0
 Tmax=300
 Tst
Xmi  WINDOW FORMAT
Xma  ↑Tstep=1
Xsc   Xmin=0
↓Ymi  Xmax=28.2
      Xscl=10
      Ymin=-2
      Ymax=4.2
      Yscl=1
```

MODE

```
Normal Sci Eng
Float 0123456789
Radian Degree
Func Par Pol Seq
Connected Dot
Sequential Simul
FullScreen Split
```

Y–

```
X1т =
Y1т =
X2т =
Y2т =
X3т =
Y3т =
X4т =
Y4т =
```

GRAPH

T

SIN

COS

– (negative sign)

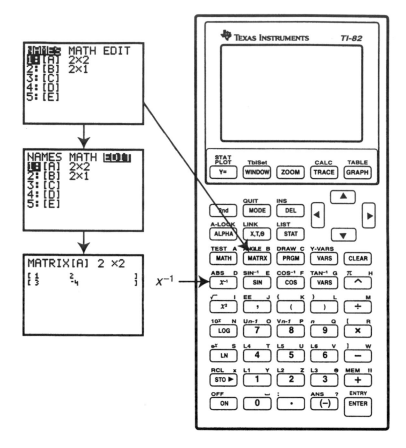

```
:NAMES MATH EDIT
1:[A]    2×2
2:[B]    2×1
3:[C]
4:[D]
5:[E]
```

```
NAMES MATH EDIT
1:[A]    2×2
2:[B]    2×1
3:[C]
4:[D]
5:[E]
```

```
MATRIX[A] 2 ×2
[ 1      2      ]
[ 3     -4      ]
```

x^{-1}

More Than Graphs, Revised Edition • ©2004 Key Curriculum Press

2nd [STAT PLOT]

```
STAT PLOTS
1:Plot1...Off
   ⌐ L1   L2     ▫
2:Plot2...Off
   ⌐ L1   L3     ▫
3:Plot3...Off
   ⌐ L1   L2     ▫
4↓PlotsOff
```

```
Plot1 Plot2 Plot3
On  Off
Type:⌐  ⌐  ⊪
     ⊞  ⊞  ⌐
Xlist:L1
Ylist:L2
Mark: ▫  +  .
```

Y=

```
Plot1 Plot2 Plot3
\Y1=
\Y2=
\Y3=
\Y4=
\Y5=
\Y6=
\Y7=
```

STAT

```
EDIT CALC TESTS
1:Edit...
2:SortA(
3:SortD(
4:ClrList
5:SetUpEditor
```

```
L1    L2    L3    1

                
L1(1)=
```

```
EDIT CALC TESTS
1:1-Var Stats
2:2-Var Stats
3:Med-Med
4:LinReg(ax+b)
5:QuadReg
6:Cu
7↓Qu
```

```
EDIT CALC TESTS
7↑QuartReg
8:LinReg(a+bx)
9:LnReg
0:ExpReg
A:PwrReg
B:Logistic
C:SinReg
```

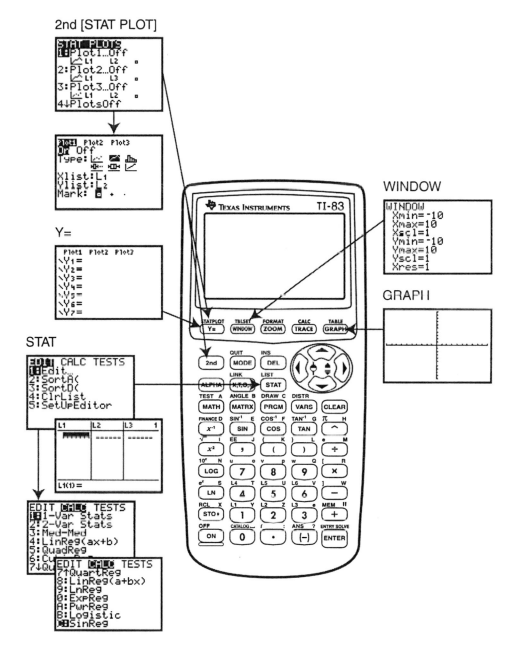

WINDOW

```
WINDOW
Xmin=-10
Xmax=10
Xscl=1
Ymin=-10
Ymax=10
Yscl=1
Xres=1
```

GRAPH

DRAW

WINDOW

```
WINDOW
Xmin=-10
Xmax=10
Xscl=1
Ymin=-10
Ymax=10
Yscl=1
Xres=1
```

MODE

```
Normal Sci Eng
Float 0123456789
Radian Degree
Func Par Pol Seq
Connected Dot
Sequential Simul
Real a+bi re^θi
Full Horiz G-T
```

2nd [FORMAT]

```
RectGC PolarGC
CoordOn CoordOff
GridOff GridOn
AxesOn AxesOff
LabelOff LabelOn
ExprOn ExprOff
```

2nd [STAT PLOT]

```
STAT PLOTS
1:Plot1...Off
   L1   L2
2:Plot2...Off
   L1   L3
3:Plot3...Off
   L1   L2
4↓PlotsOff
```

```
VARS Y-VARS
1:Window...
2:Zoom...
3:GDB...
4:Picture...
5:Statistics...
6:Table...
7:String...
```

```
PICTURE
1:Pic1
2:Pic2
3:Pic3
4:Pic4
5:Pic5
6:Pic6
7↓Pic7
```

```
DRAW POINTS STO
1:StorePic
2:RecallPic
3:StoreGDB
4:RecallGDB
```

```
DRAW POINTS STO
1:StorePic
2:RecallPic
3:StoreGDB
4:RecallGDB
```

2nd [DRAW]

```
DRAW POINTS STO
1:ClrDraw
2:Line(
3:Horizontal
4:Vertical
5:Tangent(
6:DrawF
```

```
DRAW POINTS STO
5↑Tangent(
6:DrawF
7:Shade(
8:DrawInv
9:Circle(
0:Text(
:A:Pen
```

```
DRAW POINTS STO
1:Pt-On(
2:Pt-Off(
3:Pt-Change(
4:Pxl-On(
5:Pxl-Off(
6:Pxl-Change(
7:Pxl-Test(
```

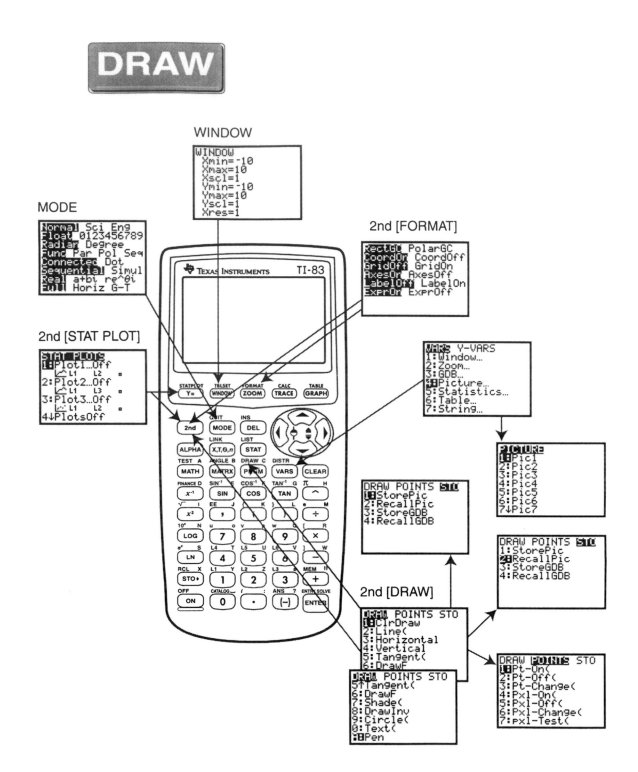

More Than Graphs, Revised Edition • ©2004 Key Curriculum Press

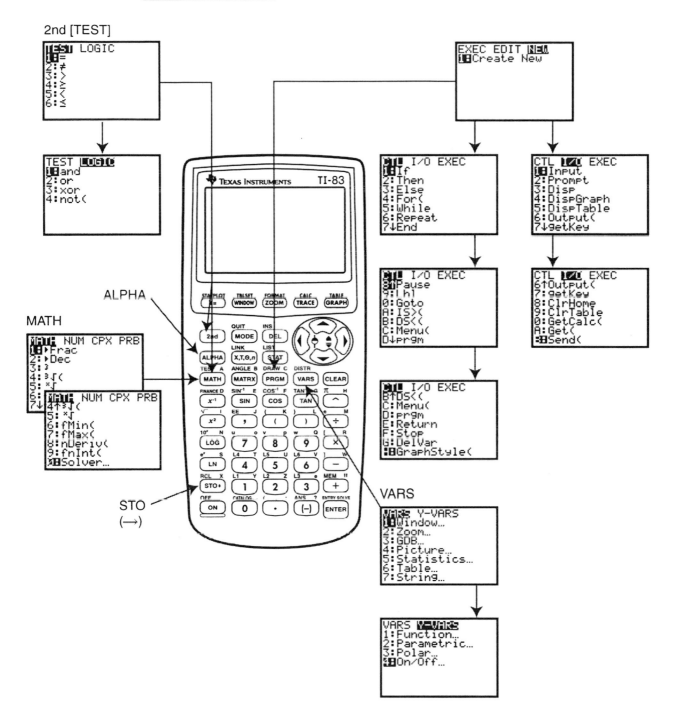

2nd [TEST]

TEST	LOGIC
1:=
2:≠
3:>
4:≥
5:<
6:≤

TEST **LOGIC**
1:and
2:or
3:xor
4:not(

ALPHA

MATH

MATH	NUM CPX PRB
1:▶Frac
2:▶Dec
3:³
4:³√(
5:ˣ√
6:↓

MATH	NUM CPX PRB
4↑³√(
5:ˣ√
6:fMin(
7:fMax(
8:nDeriv(
9:fnInt(
0:Solver…

STO
(→)

EXEC EDIT **NEW**
1:Create New

CTL	I/O EXEC
1:If
2:Then
3:Else
4:For(
5:While
6:Repeat
7↓End

CTL	I/O EXEC
8:Pause
9:Lbl
0:Goto
A:IS>(
B:DS<(
C:Menu(
D↓prgm

CTL	I/O EXEC
B↑DS<(
C:Menu(
D:prgm
E:Return
F:Stop
G:DelVar
H:GraphStyle(

CTL	I/O EXEC
1:Input
2:Prompt
3:Disp
4:DispGraph
5:DispTable
6:Output(
7↓getKey

CTL	I/O EXEC
6↑Output(
7:getKey
8:ClrHome
9:ClrTable
0:GetCalc(
A:Get(
B:Send(

VARS

VARS	Y-VARS
1:Window…
2:Zoom…
3:GDB…
4:Picture…
5:Statistics…
6:Table…
7:String…

VARS	**Y-VARS**
1:Function…
2:Parametric…
3:Polar…
4:On/Off…

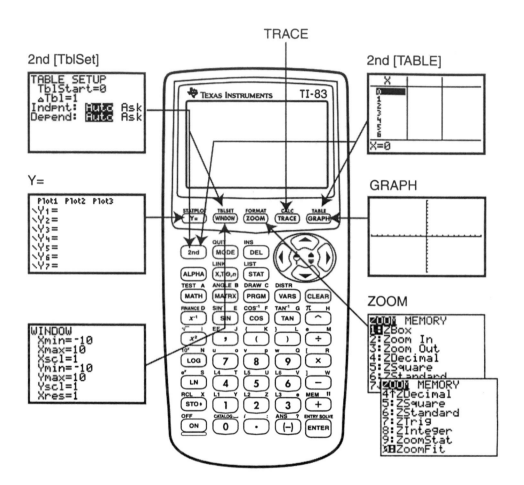

TRACE

2nd [TblSet]

```
TABLE SETUP
 TblStart=0
 ⁰Tbl=1
Indpnt: Auto Ask
Depend: Auto Ask
```

2nd [TABLE]

```
X
0
1
2
3
4
5
6
X=0
```

Y=

```
Plot1 Plot2 Plot3
\Y1=
\Y2=
\Y3=
\Y4=
\Y5=
\Y6=
\Y7=
```

GRAPH

WINDOW

```
WINDOW
Xmin=-10
Xmax=10
Xscl=1
Ymin=-10
Ymax=10
Yscl=1
Xres=1
```

ZOOM

```
ZOOM MEMORY
1:ZBox
2:Zoom In
3:Zoom Out
4:ZDecimal
5:ZSquare
6:ZStandard
7↓ZTrig
```

```
ZOOM MEMORY
4↑ZDecimal
5:ZSquare
6:ZStandard
7:ZTrig
8:ZInteger
9:ZoomStat
0:ZoomFit
```

PROB

MATH

```
MATH NUM CPX PRB
1:▶Frac
2:▶Dec
3:3
4:3√(
5:×√
6:fMin(
7↓fMax(
```

```
MATH NUM CPX PRB
1:rand
2:nPr
3:nCr
4:!
5:randInt(
6:randNorm(
7:randBin(
```

Cubed

```
MATH NUM CPX PRB
1:▶Frac
2:▶Dec
3:3
4:3√(
5:×√
6:fMin(
7↓fMax(
```

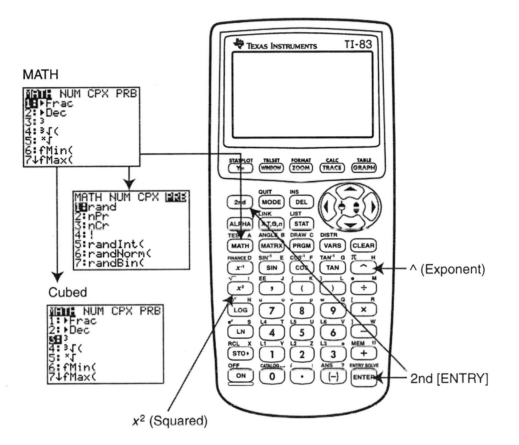

^ (Exponent)

2nd [ENTRY]

x^2 (Squared)

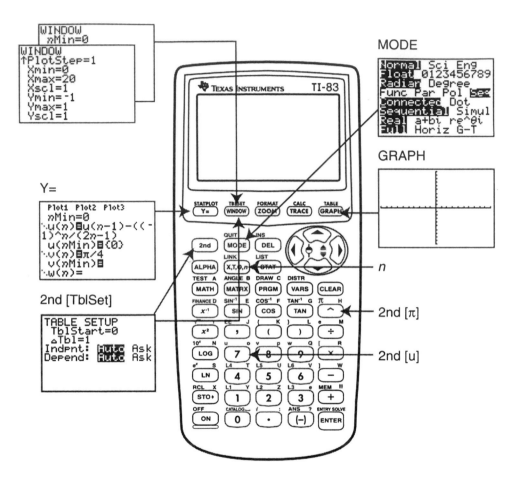

```
WINDOW
 nMin=0
```

```
WINDOW
↑PlotStep=1
 Xmin=0
 Xmax=20
 Xscl=1
 Ymin=-1
 Ymax=1
 Yscl=1
```

MODE

```
Normal Sci Eng
Float 0123456789
Radian Degree
Func Par Pol Seq
Connected Dot
Sequential Simul
Real a+bi re^θi
Full Horiz G-T
```

GRAPH

Y=

```
Plot1 Plot2 Plot3
 nMin=0
\u(n)◘u(n-1)-((-
1)^n/(2n-1)
 u(nMin)◘{0}
\v(n)◘π/4
 v(nMin)◘
\w(n)=
```

2nd [TblSet]

```
TABLE SETUP
 TblStart=0
 ∆Tbl=1
 Indpnt: Auto Ask
 Depend: Auto Ask
```

n

2nd [π]

2nd [u]

More Than Graphs, Revised Edition • ©2004 Key Curriculum Press

PARA

WINDOW

```
WINDOW
 Tmin=0
 Tmax=300
 Tstep=1
 Xmin=0
 Xmax=28.2
 Xscl=10
↓Ymin=-2
```

```
WINDOW
↑Tstep=1
 Xmin=0
 Xmax=28.2
 Xscl=10
 Ymin=-2
 Ymax=4.2
 Yscl=1
```

MODE

```
Normal Sci Eng
Float 0123456789
Radian Degree
Func Par Pol Seq
Connected Dot
Sequential Simul
Real a+bi re^θi
Full Horiz G-T
```

Y=

```
Plot1 Plot2 Plot3
\X1T=■
 Y1T=
\X2T=
 Y2T=
\X3T=
 Y3T=
\X4T=
```

GRAPH

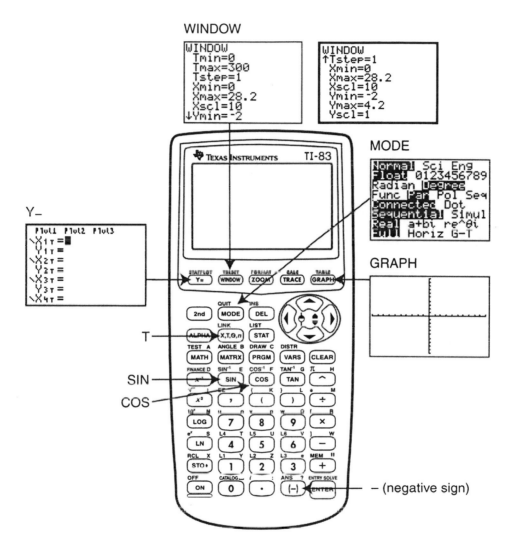

T

SIN

COS

– (negative sign)

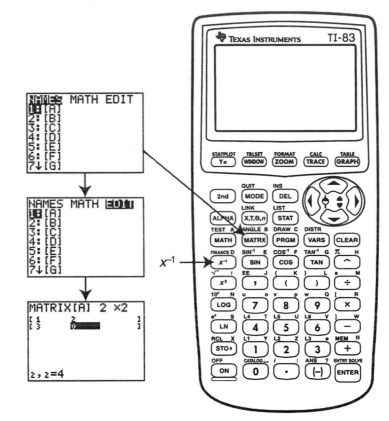

Printed in the United States
218731BV00002B/5/P

9 781559 534000